The Bar Owners' Handbook

First published in Great Britain 2019 by
Posthouse Publishing Ltd, No 2 Cleat, St Margaret's Hope, South Ronaldsay,
Orkney, KW17 2RW.
© Posthouse Publishing Ltd

A CIP catalogue for this book is available from the British Library
ISBN 978 1 903872 38 3

10 9 8 7 6 5 4 3 2 1

All rights reserved. No part of this publication may be reproduced, stored in a
retrieval system or transmitted in any form, or by any means, electronic or mechanical,
including photocopying and recording, or by any information storage and retrieval
system except as may be expressly permitted by the UK 1988 Copyright, Designs
and Patents Act and the USA 1976 Copyright Act or in writing from the publisher.
Requests for permission should be addressed to Posthouse Publishing Ltd, No 2 Cleat,
St Margaret's Hope, South Ronaldsay, Orkney,
KW17 2RW.

Disclaimer: The publishers have made every effort to ensure the accuracy of information
in the book at the time of going to press. However, they cannot accept responsibility for
any loss, injury or
inconvenience resulting from the use of information contained in this book.

Author acknowledgements
My thanks go to the Pubs Advisory Service for the facts on pub leaseholds; Ian Fozard of
Rooster's Brewery for making time to read the book; John Nunn of the Pig n Falcon, St
Neots, for sharing his cellar management skills; all case study subjects for agreeing to talk
to me; and Cat Fergusson and Anne Clarke of *On-Trade Preview* for their kindness and
generosity.

Publishers acknowledgements
The publishers would like to thank Matthew Clark Bibendum Ltd for their invaluable
help in the publishing of this book. They would also like to thank the owners of Devil's
Advocate bar in Edinburgh for the cover image.

Printed and bound in Great Britain by T.J. Internatonal Ltd.

The Bar Owners' Handbook

Ted Bruning

Contents

Foreword by Ian Fozard	vi
Introduction	1

Chapter One: Why a bar?   6
- Leasehold pubs   8
- Pubcos   9
- Brewery tenancies   11
- Franchising   12
- The free trade   15
- Shop conversions   17
- Outgoings & overheads   24
- Pricing and profit   27

Chapter Two: Planning and licensing   30
- Which comes first?   32
- Liquor licences   38
- Personal licence   42
- Training   43
- Premises licence   46
- Review and revocation   52

Chapter 3: Legal matters   54
- Recorded & broadcast music   56
- Smoking   64
- Sanitary facilities   68
- Access and equality   69
- Minors   76
- Door supervisors & security   77

Chapter 4: Beer and cider   82
- Know your beers   84
- Cask versus keg   85
- Real ale formats   88
- Cellar skills   90
- Keg, smooth and craft   97
- Bottles and cans   99

- NLA beers   101
- Cider   105
- Guest ales & promotions   107

Chapter 5: Up spirits   120
- Financial planning   123
- Gross profit   124
- The mixologist   132
- Staff training & retention   137
- The bar-back   139

Chapter 6: Wine   140
- Wine's market share   142
- Wine and food   144
- Wine training   146
- Wine service   148
- Glassware for wines   150
- Wine on tap   154

Chapter 7: Café bars   158
- Trading all day: breakfast   161
- Morning coffee & brunch   162
- Lunch   162
- Afternoon tea   164
- Coffee   165
- Tea and chocolate   168
- Soft drinks   169

8: Food   176
- Training   178
- Hygiene   181
- Environmental health inspections   185
- Health & safety in the kitchen   186
- Kitchen design & equipment   188

Waste disposal	190	
Food without cooking	193	

Appendices

Appendix I: negotiating a lease 200

Appendix II: staffing miscellany 207

Directory of services and suppliers 210

Index 222

Case studies

The Old Transporter, Henlow	18
Micro multiples	21
The Mold Alehouse	40
Room with a Brew	50
Beerhouse, Market Harborough	66
Kipps' Alehouse, Folkestone	74
Just Beer, Newark	94
The Rake, Southwark 1	116
Dare Café/A Bar Below, Leeds	130
The Wharf, Pottersbury	134
1855 Wine Bar, Oxford	152
Loungers, Bristol	170
Treacle Tap, Macclesfield	194

Foreword

By Ian Fozard, Founder of Markets Town Taverns

The British pub has been constantly evolving ever since records began. Medieval alehouses and taverns morphed into Victorian gin palaces, estate pubs and village inns. So it should be no surprise that this process of evolution continues.

Many rue the recent wave of pub closures, but in truth these are part of a continuum that stretches back many centuries. Demographics and changing social habits as well as aggressive supermarket pricing are all cited as reasons for their demise. I would add to that the huge unintended consequences of the 1990 beer orders that sucked wealth out of the pub estates of the former 'Big Six' brewers into the coffers of so-called pubcos that were in fact predatory property companies in disguise. Yet there is now strong evidence that the tide is turning. The 300-plus members of the new Micropub and Microbrewery Association are testament to that. They are at the forefront of a 'back to basics' consumer revolution that is turning its back on big business values and embracing localism, provenance and community.

In many ways CAMRA, the campaign for real ale, is responsible for this renaissance. The resurgence of cask ales and the reluctance of the pubcos to stock all but the largest national brands led to entrepreneurial individuals seeking routes to market for the new wave of beers. Indeed, being a member of CAMRA spurred me on when in 1986, together with four other local members, I started a company that over four years rejuvenated four derelict pubs in North and West Yorkshire. We reasoned that we needed to use gimmicky names to attract attention in those barren days, hence the rat theme in the pubs' names. The company was inevitably named Rodent Inns Ltd. We didn't do much to the pubs – basically a change of name and a paint job plus the installation of ten or so hand-pumps. The pubs were successful; however as we all had our own careers no one wanted to take full responsibility for them, so they were gradually sold.

I, however, was hooked, and in 1991 in my hometown of Knares-

Foreword

borough I created my first micropub – Blind Jack's – in a listed Georgian building previously home to two shops. This was a labour of love as I sought to create an alehouse atmosphere that seemed to have evolved with the building. I won a CAMRA design award for my troubles and I'm still immensely proud of Blind Jack's, even though the pressures of my day job forced its sale over 20 years ago. It's just been taken over by a young couple and given a mild makeover and looks destined to survive ad infinitum – the simple values of good ale, pleasant but basic ambience, good conversation and the absence of music are timeless.

I remained so proud at having created Blind Jack's that when I was offered the opportunity to leave my high-pressure job with a large company, I decided to return to the pub world, this time for real! In 1998, I started Market Town Taverns, which grew over 13 years to become a small chain of 15 taverns across North and West Yorkshire. Ten of these had never been pubs before; former shops, restaurants and the odd bank made excellent conversions. In almost every case the taverns were pioneering in their catchment areas in introducing independent brewers' ales coupled with decent pub fodder and good wine. I was fortunate to have received the backing of external investors and I worked bloody hard but it was hugely rewarding. And that is the underlying theme of this foreword.

It's undeniably true that the high street today has so much more choice of eating and drinking experiences for the consumer, yet many are still bland, corporate affairs. There is still, in my view, room for the entrepreneurial spirit to create their own micropub or independent bar, imbuing it with their own ideas and character and being successful. It will undoubtedly be hard work and challenging. It may not be for the faint-hearted but if you believe in your product and have the charisma, energy and determination to succeed – you usually will!

Ian Fozard
April 2019

Introduction

Introduction

This book started life as a handbook of practical advice and information for aspiring pub landlords. But I quickly came to realise that I was writing for a market that was shrinking to non-existent: hardly anyone (or hardly anyone so inexperienced as to require a vade mecum such as this) wants to run a pub these days. But, paradoxically, that's why this book is so necessary: those who do aspire to the licensed trade come from outside it and don't have easy access to the practical knowledge and skills that the trade has acquired through years or even generations of experience.

Few among us can remember a Britain in which almost every hamlet and street corner had its beerhouse where every adult male was a regular, except perhaps on club nights. Since those days, and especially since the earthquake of the 1990 Beer Orders whose aftershocks we are still feeling, the trend has been towards fewer and larger pubs, with food an ever more important part of the revenue. Big managed houses continue to appear in new housing developments. But the middle tier of general-purpose mainly leasehold pubs is feeling exactly the same squeeze that more or less wiped out family and regional brewers from the 1960s to the 1990s. And just as the disappearance of so many middle-ranking brewers made room for a kaleidoscope of small ones, so the carnage among traditional tied pubs is making room for small, narrowly-focused owner-operated bars: wine and tapas bars, licensed cafés, cocktail lounges and gin joints, craft beer bars and micropubs; and balancing all these start-ups against the continuing loss of traditional all-purpose pubs, there's a net gain of more than 2,000 a year.

The force behind this growth is freedom from having to prop up corporate stakeholders: the repair obligations, the rents, the high wholesale prices. Often, too, small start-ups are exempt from business rates. But in stripping away these overheads they do more than make themselves viable; they also further undermine generic pubs. Wine and tapas bars erode the dining trade; licensed cafés compete for what's left of the daytime trade; cocktail lounges spirit away the younger demographic. And so pubs keep closing and will continue to keep closing for as long as they are expected to fund the property companies that own them. In 10 years' time, unless these companies change their ways, the licensed trade will be unrecognisable. The leased sector will be reduced almost to nothing, and the only survivors of the 'traditional' pub trade will be giant family-oriented branded managed houses, landmark historic pubs with a big destination trade, and high-end gastropubs. For the rest, demand will be met by myriad small independent owner-operators, a situation not known in the pub trade since the 1830s. A whole new world of competition based on choice and price will open up for consumers, and genuinely independent licensees will be able to enjoy a good living and a good life without the monkey of high-rent landlords on their backs. And if that looks like a revolution, sounds like a revolution, and smells like a revolution, then it probably is a revolution.

A brief glance at the statistics will quickly show that the above is no mere hyperbole. Every year of this century, according to the British Beer & Pub Association, 1,600 pubs have closed for good. Subtracting the number of new ones that have opened, the net reduction has been more than 10,000, from 60,000 in 2000 to fewer than 50,000 in 2017. And each pub sells less beer: 23 million 36-gallon barrels or 383 barrels each in 2000; 13 million barrels or 260 each in 2016. So what's gone wrong? Well, you could argue that all that's really happening is that the licensed trade is changing its shape to fit the changing cultural and economic environment, as it always has and always will. Painful for many, but inevitable; and it's only the scale and visibility of the current shake-out that makes it so shocking. The volume of protest and vehemence of opposition to the loss of cherished local institutions ensure that the process is being played out very publicly; but whatever the strength of popular feeling, still the tide rolls in.

The crisis, if indeed there is one, stems in part from evolutionary social changes that have seen casual informal socialising go into long-term decline. These are some of them:

- Traditionally, pubs have been refuges from crowded, uncomfortable, and cheerless homes. More spacious housing, central heating, and TV and other home entertainments make staying in preferable for many.

- Greater gender equality has to a great extent dissuaded married men from regularly going out for a few beers without their wives, which was once considered quite normal.
- Many shop and office workers no longer get a full hour for lunch and no longer drink alcohol if they do. Indeed, many aren't allowed to. Sandwich shops, cafés and coffee-shops with their quicker service now outcompete high-street pubs. And a great deal of shop and office work itself has emigrated from the high street to edge-of-town retail and enterprise parks where there are few if any pubs.
- The growing price differential between on- and off-trades and the financial demands made on pubs has made them too expensive for frequent and casual use.

People feel they need a reason to go out these days, but the reason might just as well be to spend an hour on a treadmill or to share a pizza as to enjoy a couple of beers and a chat. 'Going out' is in general, therefore, more structured, more formal, and more purposeful than it used to be, and the biggest losers have been the generic traditional neighbourhood locals, mostly leased and labouring under every imaginable commercial disadvantage. Given all this, who in their right mind would want to run a pub?

There are, of course, many talented licensees running enormously successful businesses in leasehold and/or tenanted pubs, often in small chains, often with the emphasis on food. But they are generally too expensive for the small entrepreneur to go into, and often the leases won't be taken as security for loans. And since the licensing reforms of 2005 made it so much more straightforward to get a liquor licence, more and more entrepreneurs with ambitions to stand behind their own bar have started opening entirely new ones, often in shop premises, and often on a shoestring. The Micropub & Microbrewery Association reports the opening of well over 300 new cask beer-oriented bars in its 10-year existence, which taken in isolation may not sound too impressive but is only the tip of the iceberg. There are craft beer bars in every city and many towns; hip cocktail bars in Shoreditch; wine bars with mezes, tapas, and dry sherry;

microbrewery and craft distillery taps; cider barns and vineyard visitor centres; restaurants with letting rooms – and on top of all that there are bars in new-build chain hotels, in leisure centres, arts centres, sports centres, civic centres, theatres – in fact, while pub numbers continue to decline, the total number of on-licences in force is rising. At midnight on 31 March 2014, says the Home Office, there were 116,200 premises on-licences in force in England and Wales, down 1,100 on the same number a year earlier: 9,867 premises licences had been either surrendered or revoked, while 8,763 new ones had been granted. By midnight on 31 March 2016 (the publication of records having been curtailed from annual to biennial) the number had risen to 118,700. Somebody, somewhere, is making money out of running bars; for if the nation's stock of pubs is shrinking by more than 1,000 every year while the overall number of on-licences is increasing by roughly the same amount, then it follows that every year rising consumer demand for a night out is fuelling the opening of nearly 2,500 new bars. And behind every one of these new bars there stands a new licensee: the Home Office says that the number of personal licences in force in England and Wales increased by nearly 100,000 between 2009 and 2016 to 646,500. The urge to join the licensed trade is one form or another is a strong as it's ever been. But what, realistically, are the newcomers' chances?

Food and drink attracts romantics like almost no other branch of retail. Restaurateurs with a local produce fixation, organic farm shop proprietors, independent wine merchants or cheese shop owners, Q Guild butchers, artisan bakers, real ale publicans – the word "passionate" is horribly overused, but in independent food and drink retailing it finds its epiphany. And it doesn't imply starry-eyed – it can't afford to: food and drink retailing is more heavily regulated and under greater competitive pressure than almost any other trade. Still there are queues of would-be entrepreneurs who see themselves behind the bar, doing something practical to promote whatever it is they're passionate about and not only prepared but eager to face the long hours, the paperwork, the cleaning and scrubbing, not to mention the financial risk, all for the chance of seeing their belief vindicated.

Will you be one of them? If that's what you want, why not? And while this book doesn't pretend to lay out a sure route to success, it hopes to chart the reefs ahead and to help you sniff out the clearer channels. For although the sector as a whole is comfortably in growth, it still has a high churn; and the secret of success is to balance imagination and vision with practical acumen. Licensing, planning, hygiene, health and safety – deathly dull, to be sure, but it's all stuff you need to know or it will drown you. This is a practical manual that sets out to help you look before you leap, and thereby increase your already considerable chances of success.

Because business really is booming, and somewhere out there one day there'll be a flourishing micropub or cocktail lounge or wine bar packed to the gunwales with happy customers, and with your name over the door.

01

Why a bar?

Leasehold pubs	8
Pubcos	9
Brewery tenancies	11
Franchising	12
The free trade	15
Shop conversions	17
Outgoings and overheads	24
Pricing and profit	27

Case Study
Old Transporter 18

Running a pub or bar is a cherished dream for many. It probably won't make you rich (although there are always exceptions!), but it can be a very rewarding lifestyle provided that when you say you're a 'people person' you actually mean it. If you're a real ale fanatic or a farm cider zealot or an artisan spirits obsessive, or a watered-down version of any of these, it's a feasible way of making a decent living doing what you love. But how to go about it? Here are the options, and here's why you'll probably choose to open a bar.

Leasehold pubs

Until 1988, the usual gateway to the on-licensed trade was the old-fashioned brewery-owned tied tenancy. Aspirants with ambition but little or no capital could go into a tenancy in return for minimal outlay and a low rent, but they had to buy their stock exclusively from the brewery. This was, when it worked, an even-handed model that broadly satisfied both landlord and tenant; some of the surviving smaller regional brewers still offer old-style three-year fully tied tenancies. But since April 1988, when Grand Metropolitan launched its 20-year fully assignable Inntrepreneur lease, the tenancy has mostly been succeeded by variations on the long lease.

When the Inntrepreneur lease first came out it appeared to satisfy the demands of short-term tenants for greater security, greater length of tenure and an equity stake in the business, but the drawbacks soon became evident. For a start, Inntrepreneur was a full repairing put-and-keep lease, and one of the reasons it was introduced in the first place was that much of GrandMet's pub estate was in an appalling state of repair (the same was true of all the other big breweries' estates). Second, it included a minimum purchase obligation assessed by the brewery that tenants feared would be unrealistic and which, as it turned out, usually was. Third, there was an upwards-only proviso in the five-year rent reviews.

Fourth, the lease included a legal bear-trap called 'privity of contract', which made the head lessee liable for shortfalls in both rent and MPO for the full 20-year term, even if the lease was assigned. This, in the view of many licensed property brokers at the time, made the value of the lease as security more or less negligible.

As the implications sank in there was outrage among GrandMet tenants, but there was nothing they could do: they all had short tenancy agreements and as these came up for renewal they were offered long leases on a take-it-or-face-eviction basis, to which all legal challenges failed expensively. All the other major pub-owning companies quickly fell in line with similar schemes of their own, such as Allied's Vanguard lease, and it has taken many years of campaigning by lessees, the Federation of Small Business and other interested parties to get the terms of these long leases ameliorated. The 2015 Small Businesses, Enterprise and Employment Act has introduced a code of practice for multiples of 500+ pubs (there's a voluntary code for smaller chains), which even has a government appointed adjudicator to regulate and police it; but if you choose to lease your pub this is still the sort of deal you are likely to be offered. You might think that you'd be well advised to walk away, and given the possible alternative then in most circumstances you'd probably be right.

Pubcos

In 1985, after numerous failed attempts to loosen the control of Britain's six biggest brewers over the country's beer trade, the Office of Fair Trading demanded and was granted a full-scale Monopolies and Mergers Commission investigation of the brewing industry. At the time the Big Six – Bass Charrington, Allied Breweries, Whitbread, GrandMet, Courage and Scottish & Newcastle – between them brewed 75 per cent of Britain's beer and owned 34,000 pubs, just over half of the total. Regional and local brewers ranging from Greenall Whitley with more than 1,000 to Bathams with half-a-dozen, owned 12,000 between them and there were also 16,000 free houses, either belonging to small multiples or individually owner-operated.

The MMC investigation took five years and led to the 1990 Beer Orders that required the Big Six to release from tie half of all the pubs they owned above a ceiling of 2,000, which had the brewers complied would have created 11,000 additional free houses. Instead, the brewers started divesting their pub estates completely, selling them in the main to new non-brewing pub companies or pubcos, which in some cases were founded by ex-brewery executives using brewery finance and making exclusive supply arrangements with the very breweries they, the pubs, and the money had just 'separated' from! This attempt to maintain their stranglehold over the market quickly unravelled, for the Beer Orders also contained a provision allowing big brewery tenants to stock one 'guest' real ale, which instantly struck a chord both with consumers who wanted more choice and with eligible tenants who could now purchase at least one ale at free market price. Within a very short time the new pub companies realised that an exclusive diet of mass-produced national brands was not what the consumer wanted, and so they started allowing their lessees a much wider choice – albeit still purchased from the pub companies at the pub companies' prices.

In the years since then the pub companies have been in a permanent state of upheaval, facing a rapidly changing leisure market but saddled with huge debts and selling off pubs either in blocks or one at a time, merging, buying and being bought – vast but fleeting empires have risen and fallen. At their peak, Punch Taverns (now defunct, having been broken up and sold) and Enterprise Inns each owned more than 8,000 pubs. The combined holding of non-brewing pub companies has dwindled sharply since that heyday to around 20,000 – mainly because in a declining market, and under the disadvantage of having to pay inflated wholesale prices and high rents, few lessees could make enough both to pay themselves a living wage and to satisfy the demands of their landlords and their landlords' creditors.

Brewery tenancies

The brewery-owned sector that was once dominant has now shrunk to not much more than 12,000 pubs, over half of them owned by Heineken, Marston's and Greene King, and most of the rest by much smaller old-established family breweries. The majority of these are tenanted or leased, although Greene King in particular operates a great diversity of directly managed pubs, restaurants and hotels

It's in this sector where you'll find pretty much the last of the traditional tenancies, typically with a term of three to five years, with no ingoing premium or repair obligation, and in many cases no rent review either. A tenancy like this also comes with a lot more hand-holding than you'd expect elsewhere, with compulsory full training and both formal and informal support on tap, because many of the breweries involved are comparatively small. This means that every pub's contribution is significant and the company can't afford to let any of them fail.

Of course there are drawbacks. You'll most likely be tied on absolutely everything and the wholesale prices will be high, but the biggest drawback to these old-style tenancy agreements is their scarcity. The 29 surviving members of the Independent Family Brewers of Britain own fewer than 5,000 pubs between them, not all of them tenancies; and although the terms of their tenancies are in most cases short, their tenants tend to renew and pubs don't fall vacant all that often. Greene King and Marston's have fewer than 2,000 leased and tenanted pubs between them, and the smaller family brewers are unlikely to entrust one of their few tenancies to a complete novice unless there are special circumstances (e.g. you're already a TV celebrity chef with a film crew in tow). So the market isn't exactly flooded with vacant tenancies.

Franchising

Before moving off the topic of letting in all its forms, we need to touch on franchising. This looks superficially like a form of letting, but it isn't. In most but by no means all variants, it's the franchisee who supplies the premises (and who therefore isn't a rent-paying tenant) while the franchisor supplies the stock, the marketing and promotion (or at least a template for the marketing and promotion), the branding and the operating model. The franchisee's reward is usually a percentage of the take – sometimes a laughably small one – although in some models the franchisee pays a fixed fee and also various supplementary charges.

So far, this is a model that hasn't suited the pub trade for a number of reasons. One is that the potential franchisors already own all the pubs they need, and in a shrinking market the priority has until recently been to slim their estates down rather than to find new and ingenious ways of expanding them. Another is that most newcomers to the trade can convert an existing shop or other non-licensed premises (as we are about to discover) perfectly easily themselves without handing a brass farthing over to a franchisor. A third is that generic pubs don't take readily to the sort of heavy branding you tend to find in franchised operations (and, for that matter, in large managed operations such as Harvester and JD Wetherspoons): the very opposite is, in truth, the greater advantage.

Nevertheless, modified forms of franchising are beginning to creep in. A good example is Bar Sport, a US-inspired franchise of large multi-screen operations founded by ex-boxer Scott Murray. Since the investment requirement – an extremely large and expensively kitted-out premises in a prime location – all falls on the franchisee, the licence can be as little as 5 per cent of turnover after an initial fee of, in one case, £35,000. There's also a supply agreement and one assumes that this includes a little commission for the franchiser, but even so the continuing costs are low in comparison to other forms of lease or tenancy. It's the initial outlay that's daunting and for that money you might argue that you could buy your own free house. And indeed you could, but the advantage of a high-profile franchise like Bar Sport, as with McDonald's or Burger King or Budgens, is that you are stepping straight into a recognised brand with its own guaranteed demographic and you can be turning over £20,000 a week or more from week one. The scale of investment might be a deterrent and maybe you wouldn't be happy running an operation of this kind, but do visit **www.barsport.co.uk** to find out for yourself.

The more traditional pub operators are beginning to show interest in franchising now, largely as a way round the government's new code of practice (see above) and its Market Only Rent option. Marston's has been the first to dip its toe into franchising, and its package does look ideal for licensees with some experience but not much capital. The initial fee is £20,000, and the franchisee must have the same amount available as working capital. There's no rent, of course, and Marston's covers the utilities; there's also a heavy brewery input in operating and marketing support. However, the franchisee only gets to keep 20 per cent of the profit so you would need to be very confident about the outlet's trading potential before committing yourself to a five-year agreement.

Marston's also has two other rent-free packages in its

Brewery taps

Microbrewers have always acknowledged the sense in owning one or more retail outlets of their own, especially in the early days when so many pubs were brewery-tied that it was impossible for many micros to get to market. In fact the world's very first microbrewery, Selby, already owned a pub but could never stock its own ales there because the regulars only liked keg!

This little irony epitomises the fact that the relationship between microbrewers and pubs has always been complicated. On paper, the advantages are unarguable: indeed many small brewers have gone wholeheartedly into pub ownership, done well at it and turned themselves into larger and more profitable vertically-integrated companies than some of the old-established family brewers. But in practical terms running breweries and running pubs demand completely different skillsets, and many who have tried it have been overwhelmed by the difficulties of making a return on such a large investment. Others again have proved hugely successful at combining the two, either siting their breweries inside their pubs or creating bars with or without visitor centres at their breweries. In fact, for quite a long period – very roughly 2000–2010 – the brewpub was the dominant model of brewery start-up, and new ventures without at least some control over their own retail were considered very, very risky.

It was craft brewers who changed all that. Many of the pioneers did start with a pub of their own or acquired one or more very soon after opening. But the vast majority of the new generation of brewers relied for their sales on the growing excitement generated among both trade and consumers by the profusion and inventiveness they themselves created. In short, the market for craft beers has achieved the ultimate goal of making itself.

Why a bar?

> This happy state of affairs, however, will not last forever – people tire, and prescient craft brewers are already looking at modern and efficient ways of gaining more control over their own retail. The creation of an on-site brewery tap is as popular an option as ever, although for a brewery in an out-of-the way location the pickings may turn out to be slim unless the bar is part of a wider visitor attraction. The ideal compromise between an on-site tap – relatively cheap to create, easy to run and almost without overheads, but quite often on a cramped and difficult site with few chimney-pots nearby – and a full-on pub with its huge capital investment (typically a much bigger investment than the brewery itself) and vast overheads is a well-located shop conversion. It's early days yet, but 20 of the Micropub & Microbrewery Association's 300-odd members are breweries that own on-site taps, old-school pubs or micropubs... and the number is growing.

leased and tenanted division under the rather gnomic 'Retail Opportunities' banner. The ingoings are very low indeed – a £5,000 security deposit and a £360 legal fee – and virtually the only overhead the lessee has to find is staff wages. The common feature that links the pubs available for the two slightly different packages is that they're all underperforming, which will either be a challenge or a deterrent depending on your own ambition and appetite. Visit www.marstons.co.uk for information on its franchises and Retail Opportunities, and visit www.thefba.org for more information on franchises in general.

The free trade

The free trade used to be the Cinderella of the pub business. Back in the 1980s when Britain had around 75,000 pubs, more than three-quarters of them were brewery-owned, fully tied and operated either as tenancies or directly managed houses. Today, though, fewer than 12,000 of the country's 50,000-odd pubs are brewery-owned, some 18,000 belong to large non-brewing pub companies and 20,000 – the biggest tranche by a smidgeon – are free houses, either individually owner-operated or belonging to small multiples.

The growth of the free trade over the years is due to the fact that the big pub companies, saddled with debt as they are, have necessarily become risk-averse and more concerned with protecting their revenues than expanding them. Over the last quarter-century companies have divested themselves of thousands of pubs, and indeed Punch Taverns has just been split in two and sold to Heineken and a Dutch investment bank. Most of the discards have been sold in blocks to smaller pub companies or have gone for redevelopment or conversion to alternative uses, but enough have filtered through the system to increase the number of owner-operated free houses by nearly 30 per cent.

The free trade's size in terms of value, though, has grown by even more than that. This is partly because of the decline of the old system of brewery loans, which meant that most of the 'free' trade was in fact tied, and partly because of a dramatic change in the nature of the free trade itself. Whereas most free houses were once upon a time little backstreet or country beerhouses discarded by breweries as not worth the expense of maintaining, today's free house is more usually a high-throughput operation with specific expertise in, say, fine dining or real ale. Just the sort of business you probably have in mind, in fact.

But if buying a freehold pub to call your own is the classic roses-round-the-door vision, without either a big commercial mortgage or an infusion of capital such as an inheritance, house sale or redundancy cheque, it's prohibitively expensive for most of us. Of course you get a home thrown in, but in many cases it's a home whose market value you couldn't really afford on the income you'll earn from the business downstairs.

There is a third way into the licensed trade that is neither vastly expensive nor a passport to bankruptcy, and that is to rent an empty shop, buy some beer, some glasses and some chairs (optional), get yourself a licence and invite the neighbours round. This is what we now call a micropub, and it's the easiest and cheapest route to becoming the independent owner-operator of your dreams.

Shop conversions

Micropubs and their cousins – cocktail bars, tapas bars, café bars, brewery taps – are being hailed as new and revolutionary. The Micropub & Microbrewery Association now has around 300 member houses, nearly all shop conversions; but while this is potentially a revolutionary development, new it certainly isn't. Shop conversions were quite common even in 2005 when Martyn Hillier, founder and chairman of the Association, turned his off-licence in Herne village, Kent, into the Butcher's Arms. Indeed they had been the very foundation of the JD Wetherspoons Organisation; and it was Wetherspoons founder Tim Martin who, 40-odd years ago, made the micropub a legal possibility. Trained as a barrister (although he never practised) he got new licences by the score when everyone else thought it was impossible by subverting the old concept of need. Martin argued before licensing justices all over North London that 'need' could not be judged as they were in the past, simply by the local concentration of full on-licences, but by the type of businesses available to consumers in the area. And in the areas he was contesting, the existing pubs were all – not almost all, but all – shabby, run-down, Big Six-owned tenancies with little choice and high prices. Suffice it to say that he never lost a case; and although Wetherspoons has moved on somewhat

Case study – Old Transporter, Henlow
www.theoldtransporter.co.uk

Opening a micropub is like picking the bit of a pub you want to run – the public bar, in most cases – and throwing away the rest: What you're left with is the part of the pub where the money is made.

Take Steve and Jay Topham. He was an engineer and she was a business administrator, with no experience of pubs between them beyond a bit of part-time bar work years ago, when a 48m^2 shop – previously a Blockbuster franchise – came on the market in Henlow, Bedfordshire, just across the road from an enormous chain-operated steakhouse.

"What prompted us to rent the shop was an overheard conversation," says Jay. "It was a pub landlord talking about the competition from micropubs. So we looked into it and did our research and when I saw the figures I actually prodded Steve into it." Very soon after that the Old Transporter was up and running. And here's the maths. The Tophams spent a total – that's a total, mind – of £8,000 to go into the shop, including rent in advance, security deposit, stock, conversion work and professional fees. For a while they kept their day jobs but very quickly found their 24 chairs (and two sofas), four cask ales and bag/jar snacks yielded enough in 55 hours' opening a week to pay them a wage that they could live with. They have no labour costs, lower utility bills than your house and £44 a month business rates.

"It wasn't even a struggle, really," says Jay. "We'd worked out we needed to sell ten drinks an hour and we made a profit from the very start." And now that they sell spirits and lager as well as cask ale – customer demand and an appreciation of the high margin on spirits and mixers combining to triumph over ideology there – the Old Transporter's profits are even bigger.

since those early days, the business model that enabled the cheeky upstart from Barnet to outcompete its neighbours is as valid today as it was 35 years ago.

A shop conversion has proved to be the formula that answers every challenge posed by the traditional pub. Britain's pub stock is not only overburdened with unrealistic costs, it has also suffered and is still suffering from being marooned in the past. The buildings and their plots, especially those in secondary and suburban locations, are usually too big for the revenue they can be expected to generate and are generally worth more as redevelopment opportunities than as going concerns. Many of them are in completely the wrong place, too, in residential areas that used to sustain a number of pubs before regular pub-going went into steep decline, with insufficient trade to do more than tick over except on Fridays and Saturdays, and too hemmed in by neighbours to put on exciting and attractive promotional events. The business rates revaluation of April 2017, which saw rateable values soar and is being phased in at the time of writing, is certain to finish off any that are only marginally viable.

Shop conversions are far cheaper to rent, maintain and operate than big custom-built pubs that also have family homes attached. Their locations can be selected for their potential, not dictated by history. Being free of tie they can stock whatever their customers demand and buy it in cheaply on the open market to boot. And finally the architecture, décor and style of operation can diverge from tradition to suit either a particular niche market or a much more general one: simple departures from past practice such as, for instance, installing welcoming clear-glass windows instead of the rather forbidding frosted glass of the traditional pub, with coffee machines clearly on show, have proved transformative.

Tim Martin is only one expansionist entrepreneur whose chains, composed largely or entirely of conversions, have spread around the country, but for many owner-operators the aim is quite the opposite: not to be all things to all people and work flat out from 11.00 am to midnight, but to indulge a niche market, typically either craft beer or artisan spirits, on minimum outlay and overheads. This is economies of scale working backwards: Martyn Hillier's Butcher's Arms is just 12 by 14 feet (it is reputedly the smallest free house in England) and the biggest crowd that has ever squeezed in totalled 37. But it's viable because the original ingoings were negligible, the running costs are as tiny as the pub itself and because Herne has enough cask beer enthusiasts among its 7,325 inhabitants to keep Martyn's six hand-pumps busy. It's very narrowly focused, too: apart from the six cask beers it only sells bag snacks, Martyn's own pickled eggs and a token selection of wines. In short, it's perfectly balanced: it's exactly the right size and shape for its market, and its market is exactly the right size and shape for it.

To the 300 beer-oriented shop conversions of the Micropub and Microbrewery Association (at the time of writing) may be added an unknowable but much, much greater number of independently-owned shopfront (and basement!) hip city-centre craft beer or cocktail bars, boutique distillery bars, microbrewery taps, even cider barns and licensed mall cafés, that broadly speaking fit the same model. You might also include the many hotel bars leased out to third parties as quasi-independent operations, such as the Heads & Tales Bar at the Rutland Hotel in Edinburgh, which houses the Edinburgh Gin Distillery's stills. Their numbers are growing for the simple reason that any entrepreneur with the ability to add and subtract can see the financial advantages. The initial investment is low, so the price of failure need not be ruinous. The profits are not huge but then they're not shared with anybody else, so the reward for success is if not untold wealth at least a solid and unharassed living.

Case study
Micro multiples

Running a lifestyle business where you're your own boss, where you work at your own pace at an occupation you enjoy – and where you take home enough to satisfy your needs – is a dream existence for many. But the micropub model can support people with wider ambitions too. Given the incredibly low capital commitment required to open a single micropub, why not open two or even three? Can these tiny assets be worked hard enough to pay staff wages and leave something over for you too? And how do you manage your employees? These challenges face anyone running a multi-site operation of any sort. But can an entrepreneurial micropublican rise to them?

One who tried and changed his mind was experienced publican Ian Jones, who opened 'a firkin small pub' in an old heel-bar in Newent, Gloucestershire, in 2013 and naturally called it Cobblers. The original was quickly followed by two more in nearby Coleford and Cinderford. "I'd run a couple of pubs before and I would never have run another if I hadn't discovered the micropub model," Ian says. "After a while I decided to open the other two just to see if I could make them work."

Financially, they did. Small but popular, and with vanishingly low overheads, they generated enough cash to pay the staff Ian hired and still make a good profit. But managing them at a distance proved frustrating. "It wasn't that the staff were dishonest," he says. "I did regular till and stock checks and they weren't handing out free drinks or anything like that. But they wouldn't do things the way I like them. I have a golden rule: no drinking at work. But I would turn up and find them with a drink. And they were supposed to finish the cleaning before opening, but I would find them still hoovering after the doors had opened."

The Cinderford and Coleford branches were taken off Ian's hands by regular customers Greg Daniels and Steph Rogers, who had been looking for a suitable site in the area but happily settled for two. The pair rebranded their acquisitions as the Dog Houses and they run one each, so they have no problems of supervision. And like Ian they have no problem with profitability – so much so that they are looking for Dog House number three. One essential, says Greg, is that the sites shouldn't be too tightly controlled or too heavily branded. "It's important to maintain the site's individuality," he says. "Each Dog House will have to be true to its customers and respond to what they want. And one of the joys of being so small is that it's possible to have that individual relationship with your locals".

Dave and Nicola Holland also run two micropubs, the Wight Bear in Southbourne, Bournemouth, which they opened in 2015, and the Saxon Bear 10 miles away in Christchurch, which followed a year later. Dave was previously in the property development business and has lived in the area for 30 years; what first brought him to apply his business acumen to the bar trade was a love of beer coupled with knowledge of the local market. That was soon followed by an appreciation of the virtues of the micropub model.

The couple, both beer-lovers, were taking time out to tour the south coast seeking out micropubs. "We saw about a dozen and I thought the whole concept was just brilliant," says Dave. "It brings new people into the trade and there's a love of good beer at its core. We wanted someone to open one near us and when nobody did we decided to do it ourselves!"

The Wight Bear is a bit more high-concept than some micropubs: as well as local real ales and traditional ciders, the Hollands have managed to source almost an entire range of spirits from local distillers and blenders: Black Cow whey vodka from Beaminster;

Conker gin from Bournemouth and Pothecary gin from Christchurch; and Golden Cap, a very superior whisky custom-blended for Palmer's of Bridport. There's also locally made wine from the Furleigh Estate near Lyme Regis.

Although looking for a second pub wasn't part of the original plan, the Wight Bear soon became so popular that the Hollands started thinking about expanding. In fact, the Wight Bear was doing such good business that the acquisition and kitting-out of the Saxon Bear was funded out of cash flow, and the turnover and GP are so high that each pub has its own salaried designated premises supervisor, both of them qualified and experienced. The supervisors, says Dave, have been key crucial to the pubs' success. "The real attraction of a micropub is the person who runs it," he says. "People don't buy from formats – people buy from people."

For Greg and Steph, and the Hollands, building up a little empire of micropubs wasn't part of the strategy, and there are still very few multiple micropub operations around. But to a well-funded entrepreneur the prospect of investing a mere £100,000 or so in a chain of five or six popular bars – every one of which might return a net profit of £20,000 or more – is bound to be very, very alluring. Could that entrepreneur be you?

Outgoings and overheads

Before you actually start trading – and long before you've reached this point in the proceedings, hopefully – you'll have sat down with your calculator and worked out whether you're actually going to make any money. Of course, the calculations are going to be very different from case to case, but here's an outline of the considerations that are making bars a more popular option than old-style pubs with so many prospective licensees.

For a start, ingoings are exponentially lower. There's no SAV, no fixtures and fittings, no goodwill, no premium – just a security deposit, very little in the way of professional fees, minimal insurance, six weeks' rent in advance, new stock and fitting-out. You can equip a cellar or still-room with a good-as-new chiller, cask-tilts, a keg store and a sack truck for £1,400 plus VAT and buy a dishwasher, ice-maker and two double-door bottle-chillers for the bar for about the same using a website such as www.second-hand-pub-equipment.co.uk, of which there are many. Even including tables and chairs and the bar counter itself, you can quite possibly get away with spending less than £10,000 – many have – and if you use a credit card you won't even have to pay that for a month, by which time the cash will be flowing.

When it comes to overheads, small is more beautiful still. Like any free trader you can shop around for your stock, so you'll buy cheaper than your tied counterpart. Your rent will be low because the premises are small and there's no licensee's accommodation to pay for. Then there are business rates. The rateable value of a full-sized pub will in most cases be at or above the level, set at £51,000 at the time of writing, where the licensee has to pay at the full business multiplier of 47.9p in the pound. The low rateable value of your shop, however, will almost certainly mean you are assessed at the small business multiplier of 46.6p and may also be entitled to a discount; it might possibly even fall below the level – £15,000 at the time of writing – at which you are excused business rates altogether. Without a kitchen and amusement machines your utilities will probably be much the same as they are at home, although chiller cabinets, ice machine and a glasswasher can consume a fair amount of juice. Go three-phase to keep the costs down and if you are using electric cookers, fridges, freezers and dishwashers it might well be worth buying through a utilities broker.

Insurance is another expense that can't be left out of the cash flow projection in your business plan. Naturally you will insure your premises, stock and fixtures and fittings in the normal way; you will also, if you have any sense, insure yourself against sickness or injury; and public liability including product liability insurance is, although not compulsory under the law, more or less a given. Your most important insurance policy, though, is the one that protects your staff.

After rent, your biggest overhead may very well be staff costs, conventionally reckoned at 30–35 per cent of gross profit. If you and a partner are running a fairly straightforward micropub opening noon–10.00 pm Tuesday–Saturday plus noon–3.00 pm Sunday, you can probably get away without help: 53 hours between two is fairly leisurely by some standards, although of course there's cleaning, stocktaking and other chores to be done outside of opening hours. If you're running a more intensive operation – a city-centre cocktail bar, say – then the maths changes completely. You have to pay at least minimum wage as well as employer's National Insurance at 13.8 per cent for workers who put in more than 18 hours (and as a result you will find that two part-timers are about £1,000 a year cheaper than one full-timer), and Employer's Liability Insurance is compulsory with an eye-watering fine for dodging it.

Employer's Liability Insurance has been a statutory requirement since 1969. You are required to insure your workforce up to a minimum cover of £5 million (although £10 million is more usual) because the policy is also required to cover all possible legal fees and court costs. Failure to comply incurs – theoretically at least – perhaps the heaviest fine of all in the entire compliance jungle: £2,500 for every single day you trade without cover (plus another £1,000 if you fail to display your policy either on your website or as a physical poster)! So make sure your EL insurance is valid the moment you take on your first member of staff. If you have a coherent health and safety policy in place – i.e., if you're a good risk – your premiums needn't be astronomical: by shopping around you should find all the insurance you'll need for less than £1,000 a year. However, what really irks many small businesses about your health and safety policy is that it's so time-consuming, fiddly and bureaucratic.

The up-to-date documentation employers are strictly expected to be able to produce at the drop of a hat includes:
- Policy and procedures
- Risk assessments and control measures implementation
- Use of safe systems of work/permit to work systems
- Training courses/records
- Accident reports/analysis
- Health surveillance records
- Statutory inspections
- Safety committee meetings minutes
- Occupational health action plans.

You therefore need either to be very well organised yourself or have a very well-organised right-hand person in the office, or have a consultant set up all your systems and instruct you in proper record-keeping. But as a small business you shouldn't find occupational health and safety as big an ogre as it looks, and of course if you have no employees it's something that need hardly worry you at all.

Pricing and profit

How about income, then? Well, if your mainstay is draught beer and cider, you shop carefully and you serve little or no food, you can reckon on a gross profit of 60 per cent – that is, £60,000 in every £100,000 turnover. But wines, spirits and soft drinks all have much bigger mark-ups than beer: for instance, a £15 bottle of spirits containing 28 measures @ £3 gives you a profit of £69. So if your sales mix includes a modest proportion of wines, soft drinks and spirits your gross profit will be even higher; and as it's all paid for cash on the nail you're guaranteed a healthy cash flow.

However, 60 per cent of nothing is still nothing, so leaving percentages aside, can the tiny turnover yield enough actual cash for you to live on? Well, there's a lot of assumptions in the following, but you should be able to juggle them to fit your circumstances.

Let's say you and your partner, if you have one, live modestly and can manage on about one and a half times the national average wage between you. Your net profits target is therefore £40,000. Your annual business overheads (without staff) might be in the order of: utilities, £1,000 odd; insurance premiums, bank charges and professional fees £1,000 at most (less if you don't take plastic). At the low level of ingoings you paid upfront you probably won't have a loan to repay; in a rented premises depreciation isn't an issue; the occasional lick of paint or replacement chair should be negligible; and you are most likely to be exempt from business rates. That leaves the rent, which of course will vary enormously from location to location. You should, however, be able to find 750 sq ft in a secondary location almost anywhere outside London for £18,000 a year.

That all comes to £60,000, and assuming your gross profit really is 60 per cent then to reach your target your turnover need only be £100,000 a year, or £2,040 a week (assuming you take your three weeks off in January or February, when trade is negligible) or £38 an hour. Even at £3.50 a pint, which is on the low side at the time of writing, you therefore need to average 10–11 sales an hour to hit your target. If you can't do that, you may well be in the wrong job.

The Bon Vivant Group

A collection of quality, independent venues.
Restaurants, Bars, Wine & Spirit Merchant.

info@bonvivantedinburgh.co.uk   0131 225 3275

THE BON VIVANT
EST. 2008

THE BON VIVANT'S COMPANION
EST. 2011

The DEVIL'S ADVOCATE
BAR & KITCHEN

EL CARTEL
CASERA MEXICANA

LADY LIBERTINE

THE REGISTER CLUB

02

Planning and licensing

Which comes first? 32
Liquor licences 38
Personal licence 42
Training 43
Premises licence 46
Review and revocation 52

Case Studies
The Mold Alehouse 40
Room with a Brew 50

It may be obvious but it's still worth emphasising: the essence of a shop conversion is the conversion of a shop. So let's skip the pleasurable although often frustrating business of house-hunting and jump to the point where you have found, in or perhaps just off a high street near you or in a neighbourhood parade or in a village whose last pub has closed, a large-ish empty shop or office that would make an ideal bar. You have a satisfactory lease at a rent you can afford. You have enough capital to kit it out, with some left over for a float, albeit a modest one (but then this is, after all, going to be a cash business). The two things you need before opening are your premises licence and change of use permission. Both should be fairly straightforward, although of course there's many a slip between cup and lip. But which should you apply for first?

Which comes first?

The professional consensus is that under normal circumstances the planning application, which is in theory the less complicated of the two, should come before the premises licence. This isn't always the case, and it varies from council to council, but most licensing committees prefer the premises in question to have its use status already confirmed, and since the planning process requires much the same consultation as the licence application does, you might as well get it done first. Then, if you do get your change of use consent, the licensing process is more than half completed; if you don't, you can cut your losses without wasting any more time and energy. It may well be the case, though, that the property owner is in a hurry to get you moved in and paying rent, in which case you'll have to run both applications simultaneously. If that turns out to be necessary keep all the relevant officials – fire, police and other interested bodies as well as council planning and licensing officers – up to date with what's going on and never be afraid to ask for their advice.

Planning and licensing

Change of use permission

Under the Use Classes Order 1987 commercial premises fall broadly into five categories. A1 is shops, A2 most types of office, A3 restaurants and cafés, A4 pubs and bars and A5 takeaways. In most cases you are allowed to change the use of the premises from one category to another without change of use permission, but there are two exceptions – and guess which they are. Yes, you're right – you can turn a shop into an office or a bistro, you can turn an office into a shop or a bistro and you can turn a bistro into a shop or an office, all without troubling the town hall. But because of public order concerns, you need change of use consent to turn an office, shop or bistro into a bar or takeaway.

It shouldn't usually be too complicated – in theory, anyway. The modest dimensions of the premises and the neighbourhood's classification in the Local Development Framework (see below) should allay the planning officer's reservations about noise and nuisance; and although the planners won't officially take your premises licence application into consideration, if you can demonstrate that you plan to operate a small, quiet neighbourhood bar serving products aimed at the older and/or more discerning end of the market and closing at 10.00 pm, they'll normally regard your change of use application sympathetically. It will help your cause enormously if you raise all these matters unprompted and respond positively to any suggestions the officer makes, and even more if you thoroughly canvass and/or mailshot neighbouring residences well in advance. That doesn't mean anything will go through on the nod, and there have been times when all the would-be licensee's promises and blandishments have failed to overcome the neighbours' reservations (see case study below), but planning officers are not ideologically opposed to the very existence of licensed premises – and indeed planning law does theoretically at least require planning authorities to make provision for commercial facilities – and will usually be as helpful as you'll allow them to be.

If your plans are more ambitious than turning a shoe-shop into a bar – if you plan to carve a new bar out of old farm buildings or railway buildings or canal-side warehouses, say – then your planning application becomes more complicated. Getting the whole process under way will involve you in two processes: evaluating the building itself and evaluating its surroundings. Obviously it's wise to carry out this exercise as thoroughly as possible before signing a lease or making a purchase – you don't want to be stuck with premises you can't use or face a long hard battle to get your application through before you can start trading.

As far as the building is concerned, there's quite a long list of boxes to tick. If it's an older property, is it listed (if it is, see Listed Building Consent and case study below)? As for its surroundings, is it in a conservation area, an Area of Outstanding Natural Beauty or a National Park? How good is the vehicle access? Is there room on the site for delivery vehicles to manoeuvre if required? How many traffic movements on and off site do you envisage? Can it jump through all the relevant health and safety hoops? Can you control noise and emissions to the satisfaction of local residents?

Getting planning permission is – supposedly, at least – somewhat more straightforward these days than it used to be; and thanks to the web, it's also much easier to get the information you need than it was. At **www.planningportal.gov.uk** you'll find a pretty exhaustive guide to planning matters; it even enables you to apply online and includes a fee calculator to help you work out roughly how much the council will charge you. Another useful link is to the Royal Town Planning Institute's site, which includes a list of planning consultants one of whom, Ian Butter, has a truly excellent guide to your planning needs on his site: **www.ruralurbanplanning.co.uk**.

In law councils have to determine your application within eight weeks of receiving it, although they do have the power to extend the permitted period under certain circumstances. If they do, you can appeal to the Secretary of State, but it's rather self-defeating as the appeal will almost certainly take longer than the council would. So if you want your application to be determined as quickly as possible – and if you want to be sure of getting the right result – then everything hinges on thorough preparation and good communication. What this means is that the whole planning process may take longer than eight weeks, but – just as with your premises licence application – the real work will have been done before your application actually goes in.

Your first job is to check the relevant sections of the Local Development Framework thoroughly. This is available from the city, borough or district council, or on its website. Unfortunately it's not a single document, but a collection of them: however the site should be fairly easy to navigate. The LDF is divided into two sections: general policy across the whole district and more specific policies location by location. Armed with this information, you should at least be able to tell whether the building you have your eye on is likely to be acceptable for A4 use. Some council websites are less clear than others, but are still far from impenetrable, and once all the documents are located, LDFs are fairly straightforward and easy to understand.

The planners' main concern, after the suitability of the building itself, will be the impact of your business on its neighbours, especially if there are any residents in the immediate area. This concern is partly but not entirely met by the LDF's approved uses for the locality. But your planning officer will also be interested in noise, smells and other emissions, waste collection and any changes you propose to make to the appearance of the building, particularly if you will need highly visible equipment such as extractors.

A large part of the process involves consultation, and not just with the neighbours. Of course, you will have to advertise your application both in the local press (another expense!) and on the application premises to give them the chance to object if they fear your plans will threaten the 'amenity' of the area. But it will help you if you do more than the bare minimum. Write to them; meet them; speak to them. Develop a genuine interest – and make sure they know you're taking genuine interest – in their concerns and their suggestions. But the grounds on which they can object are limited by statute, and the planning authority is specifically instructed (see the Planning Portals website again) that the mere number of objections is irrelevant. It doesn't (or shouldn't) make the slightest difference if every neighbour within three-quarters of a mile just doesn't want your property to be a pub: it's your property, not theirs, and their views should only be taken into account if they have valid concerns about noise and other nuisance. In reality, planning officers and even more the elected members of the planning committee, will put undue weight on numbers: if there are very great numbers of residential objections, however spurious, you might think about cutting your losses and looking elsewhere.

As with your premises licence application, though, the main consultation will be with statutory bodies: the local council's own environmental health department, the county council as highways authority, the police and fire services, the parish council and the Health and Safety Executive. This is the part of the process that really takes time, and it's these agencies that are likeliest to have objections. However, you should be able to combine your planning and licensing consultations, and if your application conforms to the LDF and is made out thoroughly and in proper form (and with professional advice if you feel it necessary), you should hopefully clear this last hurdle and start trading.

Planning and licensing

> ### Listed buildng consent
>
> You may very well need another, more difficult, permission, too: older buildings are frequently protected by statutory listing and need listed building consent before any alterations that will affect their appearance or character can be made. Strictly speaking, this is not part of your change of use application as it's covered by different laws, but in practice the two applications can be submitted at the same time. They remain separate applications, though, and the outcome of one doesn't affect the outcome of the other. You can be granted listed building consent on the grounds that your proposals don't affect the building's character, but still be refused change of use permission on the grounds that, say, vehicle access is inadequate. Refusal of either application can be challenged, so if you're knocked back on one but get through on another, the game's not necessarily up. You can either appeal or revise the failed planning application (in consultation with the relevant planning officer, naturally) and reapply.

Appeals

The obvious thing is to appeal, and you have six months from the rejection of your application to do so. Once again, the Planning Portal contains all the details you need – you can even appeal online! They are handled by the Planning Inspectorate, which appoints an independent inspector to whom you can state your own case and comment on the planning authority's statement of case. The inspectorate also appoints a case officer who will help you by telling you what documentation to present and when, although when dealing with unfamiliar, complex and jargon-ridden rules and regulations you may well feel you need the advice of an experienced surveyor or planning consultant.

An appeal is the only way to overcome refusal of listed building consent, but if you are refused change of use permission, a quicker and cheaper option is to find out what the council didn't like about your application, amend it accordingly and then resubmit. If you do this within 12 months there will be no fee, and as objections to the original application are considered to have been dealt with already they can't be submitted again. This is the way large corporations wear down local objectors – they simply present slightly altered applications again and again and again until their opponents either run out of new objections or are simply too worn out to continue. That's perhaps not quite what you have in mind, but if you have been refused on minor or technical grounds this is the simplest solution.

Once you have been granted planning permission, you have three years to act on it before it expires. You probably won't need that long, though!

Liquor licences

As the proud owner of your very own micropub/cocktail lounge/café bar, the one thing you can't do without is your licence. Or to be more accurate, the two things you can't do without are your licences – one for you and one for the bar. A bit of background.

Before the 2003 Licensing Act came into force (in 2005, as it happens, but never mind that), liquor licensing was a jungle of applications and requirements administered by magistrates qualified for the job only by their respectability. Brewster sessions, transfer sessions, protection orders, supper hours certificates, holiday extensions, music and dance licences, proliferation and need – licensing was a red-tape generator that kept justices' clerks and specialist surveyors and solicitors in gravy for generations, while obliging licensees to hang around magistrates' courts when they could have been working. That's all gone now, because the 2003 Act was one of those rare pieces of legislation that was genuinely revolutionary. Sweeping away age-old encrustations of rules and regulations, it brought licensing up to date, encouraging entrepreneurship while ensuring that pubs connected with their communities and lightening the burden of bureaucracy. The Act's main provisions were threefold. You need to know them all, so here they are.

Most prominent was the abolition of permitted hours, castigated as '24-hour opening' by the media and widely predicted to result in ubiquitous drunken rioting and looting, as well as the general breakdown of civilisation. In the event few pubs wanted 24-hour opening and few licensing committees would have let them have it anyway. The underlying hope was that city-centre clubs and bars would stagger their closing hours so that hordes of drunken youths wouldn't pour out on to the street all at the same time, which didn't happen because every club wanted to be the last to close and no customers wanted to go home until there was no more drink to be had. For the record, at the time of writing fewer than 8,000 24-hour licences are in force, 47 per cent at hotels, 28 per cent at off licences (mainly supermarkets and forecourt shops), 14 per cent at takeaways (many of them not being liquor licences) and just 11 per cent at pubs and bars. All the same, and even away from town centres, the peak trading period insensibly shifted from 11.00 pm to midnight and beyond, much to the annoyance of neighbours. In response, the government has given councils power to impose Early Morning Alcohol Restriction Orders requiring all pubs in a designated area to close between midnight and 6.00 am. Anyone can apply for an EMRO, including the police and local residents, and there has to be a hearing at which all parties can put their cases. But to put matters into context, and as you will see if you read on, the real prize has not been all-night opening but all-day opening.

The next big change was to transfer the licensing function from magistrates to councils, leading to much wider and

Case study
The Mold Alehouse

Mold is one of those surprising towns you find throughout Scotland and Wales which, although small, turn out to be important administrative centres and come equipped with a full set of architecturally quite impressive municipal and commercial buildings. Having been the county town of Flintshire for time out of mind (and, briefly, of Clwyd) Mold has a centre dignified by a clutch of listed buildings, including a grand town hall and, opposite it, Eagle Chambers, once the regional office of the *Chester Chronicle* and now home of the Mold Alehouse.

Eagle Chambers is a rather grandiose but fanciful Edwardian pile with a sombre upper storey of plum-coloured brick and terracotta and a ground floor smothered in pale freestone trimmings: pilasters, cornices, parapets, keystone arches, quoins and other such folderols. When Gareth and Rebecca Jones came along looking for a suitable clay in which to plant their micropub dream it seemed ideal: unusual, striking, memorable, and, as in its immediate past incarnation it had been a café, not too difficult to convert. But given its listed status, and the fact that the first floor had been converted into flats, the Joneses knew that getting the premises licence and change of use permission might be tricky. So they did exactly the right thing: they went out and talked to people. "It wasn't too challenging, actually," says Gareth. "We tried to anticipate what concerns all the different interested parties were likely to raise and deal with them in advance. We met all the neighbours before we even put any applications in and agreed on last orders at 10.00 pm and closing at 10.30 pm. We had environmental health round to advise on food hygiene, and the police licensing officer came and only made one suggestion, which was that we install CCTV."

The council's conservation officers also had only one suggestion before granting listed building consent, which was that the vents from the extractor in the still-room should be moved so they couldn't be seen from the street. And they were more than pleased when the Joneses had the floating ceiling taken out, because that revealed the arched tops of the original sash windows. The upstairs neighbours were pleased too, because it meant the ceiling could be soundproofed (even though it turned out to be unnecessary in the end).

So there you have it: a holy trinity of co-operative officials, reasonable neighbours and diligent applicant meant that everything went smoothly. Bit of a non-story, really. Which is just fine...

more detailed public consultation. The Act not only requires licensees to understand and uphold the four key public policies (see below), it also ensures that the police and fire services are involved in the agreement of conditions, and that neighbouring businesses, residents and public institutions – mainly schools and hospitals – are allowed a say in how the premises is operated.

The third and perhaps most significant reform was to split liquor licences in two, so that you now need both a personal and a premises licence. Ill-informed critics claimed that this would merely add another layer of bureaucracy to an already enormous pile; in fact, it did the opposite, principally by ending the cumbersome old system of licence transfers and making it much easier for licensees to migrate from pub to pub without having to make two court appearances at each move.

Personal licence

The first thing you need, then, is a personal licence issued by your local council, which at the time of writing costs £37. It's a very straightforward business, not much more involved than filling in a simple form, but before you can apply you will need a National Certificate for Personal Licence Holders. To get one, you need to attend a one-day training course which has a 40-question multiple-choice exam at the end. This shouldn't cost more than about £250–£300, and as the British Institute of Innkeeping accredits some 500 training providers who run courses at over 5,000 locations all over the country, it shouldn't be too hard to shop around. To find one, visit **www.biiab.org**. The test, it has to be said, is astonishingly easy.

Once you've got your certificate but before you apply for your licence, you will need a Disclosure and Barring Service check (formerly the Criminal Records Bureau check), which costs £26. As a self-employed person you can only request the basic check. You can ask for an application form online at **www.gov.uk**, although the form has to be printed off, filled out in black ink and returned by post along with two passport photos certified by a person of standing. You can download the licence application form from your council's website.

Training

Of all the white-collar professions, the licensed trade has traditionally been among the least skilled. Like much small independent retail until surprisingly recently, its principal recruiting grounds were young working-class men who were too ambitious and too bright for factory fodder but not quite ambitious and bright enough for a clerical or managerial career; alternatively they might be older working-class men, typically ex-servicemen or policemen, who were pensioned off at a comparatively young age. But the licensed trade was exceptional in that the ingoings required were beyond even the latter with their pensions and savings. So the brewers set them up as tenants, charging them only fixtures and fittings and stock at valuation but tying them for every product they sold – wines, spirits and soft drinks that were in many cases often made at the brewery itself, as well as beer. Tenants with so few choices to make needed little training. Beyond basic cellar skills and bookkeeping, there was little to learn that could not be picked up on the job: tenants were flung in at the deep end with no intellectual weaponry beyond common sense.

How things have changed! Here, to illustrate the breadth of skills required by a truly professional modern licensee, is a list of the main qualifications offered by the British Institute of Innkeeping Awarding body:

- Award for Personal Licence Holders (APLH)
- Award for Designated Premises Supervisors (ADPS)
- Award in Beer and Cellar Quality (ABCQ)
- Award in Drugs Awareness (ADA)
- Award in Licensed Retailing (ALR)
- Award in Responsible Alcohol Retailing (ARAR)
- Award for Licensing Practitioners (Gambling) ALP(G)
- Profitable Business Portfolio (PBP)
- Level 3 Award in Licensed Hospitality
- Level 3 Certificate in Licensed Hospitality

None of these qualifications is mandatory apart from the APLH, and the licensed trade remains, in terms of formal qualifications at least, relatively unskilled. To protect their investment both non-brewing pub companies and breweries these days mostly insist that new lessees should undergo a certain amount of formal training before taking over. The courses they offer are not free, but in most cases they're not expensive either: Marston's mandatory Pre-Entry Awareness Training, for instance, costs only £75, and more advanced training is generally offered at a discount. Qualifications in the commercial and business aspects of running a pub apart, there's also an awful lot a licensee needs to know about legal requirements and compliance: many of them are detailed in the next chapter. Food hygiene is an obvious area of concern here, and is very strictly regulated. Employment law can also be an absolute minefield that you need to be able to navigate before taking on staff.

If you get into trouble – or indeed if you want to avoid getting into trouble in the first place – over any of these regulatory questions, the first place to turn to should be your professional body or trade association. Membership of the BII and/or the Federation of Licensed Victuallers (**www.flva.co.uk**) or, in Scotland, the Scottish Licensed Trade Association (**www.theslta.co.uk**) is invaluable since they not only

Planning and licensing

offer legal and regulatory advice, but they're also run in the main by experienced licensees whose first-hand knowledge makes them as much to be valued as professional advisers. It's also useful to join the Federation of Small Businesses.

You should also keep yourself abreast of the latest developments in the trade at large by subscribing to both *The Morning Advertiser* and *Inapub*, either in printed form or online, and possibly *Caterer & Hotelkeeper* as well. The long hours a licensee spends in the kitchen or behind the bar can be very isolating, so belonging to a trade association and subscribing to the trade press will help you to maintain a connection to the world beyond your front door that is often a lifesaver.

Designated premises supervisors

Under Section 19 of the 2003 Act, every premises that sells alcohol must have on its licence a named Designated Premises Supervisor, who must be a personal licence holder. The DPS should normally be in control of, or should be formally conversant with, the day-to-day management of the premises, and his or her primary role is to be a contact point with the licensing authority and the emergency services. The DPS is also responsible for ensuring that the three Mandatory Conditions that are now included in the Act are observed (see below).

The DPS needn't be on the premises at all times but must be contactable. When the DPS goes on holiday he/she should inform the police, fire service and licensing authority when and where they're going and when they expect to get back, but their relief manager doesn't have to be their named DPS. A licensed premises needs only one DPS, but a personal licence holder can be the DPS of more than one premises.

If this sounds pretty much like a description of the premises licence holder to you, well, in the vast majority the two are one and the same. The existence of a separate DPS is only really required as a deputy for a multiple licensee whose pubs are some distance apart or who isn't closely involved in their day-to-day running.

Premises licence

Now that you have both your personal licence and your planning permission, it's time to apply for your premises licence. This application may have been running in tandem with your change of use application; but anyway, here's how you get one.

When premises licences were introduced, a decision was made to simplify the whole process by sweeping away all the previous categories – full on-licences for pubs, restricted on-licences for restaurants, off-licences, gaming licences, cinema licences, promoter's licences – and instead creating a single umbrella premises licence that would cover all licensable activities. As a result there's a fearsome-looking 16-page form to fill in, but if you download it from your local council's website and give it a good read you'll see that most of it isn't relevant to you at all; and the trickier sections, such as those to do with carrying out the four licensing objectives, will have been covered in your personal licence holder's training course. There's a fee of £100–£2,000 depending on the rateable value of the premises: as your premises will almost certainly be at the bottom of the rateable value league table your fee ought to be the minimum.

Despite appearances, the form is actually fairly simple – you shouldn't need a solicitor to help you fill it out, and it should only take you a day or at most two. But the actual form filling is only the final part of the process. You will also need to advertise your application as prescribed by the licensing authority (which is not a new requirement); you will need to submit an accurate and intelligible plan of the

Planning and licensing

Four objectives, three conditions

The 2003 Act enshrines four licensing policy objectives that you should know by heart. They are:
- The prevention of crime and disorder
- Public safety
- The prevention of public nuisance
- The protection of minors.

In Scotland there is a fifth objective, the protection of public health, which may be introduced in the rest of the UK before long.

Three Mandatory Conditions have subsequently been added, the second of which you might want to pin up somewhere prominent! They are:
- That there should be no irresponsible promotions that involve drinking games, unlimited or unspecified quantities of alcohol for a single set price, free alcohol as a prize or any promotional material that condones, encourages or glamorises antisocial behaviour or portrays drunkenness favourably.
- That water, either tap or bottled, should be freely available to customers who ask for it. Helpfully, the accompanying notes make it clear that the term 'customer' here carries 'its plain English definition', so that if someone already on the premises asks for water they must be given it, but if the local cycling club pulls up outside all demanding water without intending to buy anything, you may refuse... politely or otherwise.
- That there must be a workable policy to verify the age of customers who appear to be under 18. Acceptable ID should generally bear the customer's photograph and date of birth along with a hologram (preferably the Home Office's own Proof of Age Standards Scheme or PASS hologram). Both full and provisional driving licences are acceptable POA, as are valid passports.

> Expired passports are more problematical because in the case of, say, a 22-year-old, the photo on the passport may well be that of a 12-year-old!
>
> It almost goes without saying that it is illegal to knowingly sell alcohol to anyone who is drunk. It is also illegal to allow alcohol to be sold to someone who is drunk. Whoever sells the alcohol, the premises licence holder and the DPS could face prosecution, a fine of £1,000 and revocation of their personal licence. It is also an offence for a person to knowingly get, or try to get, alcohol for a drunk person on licensed premises.

premises, although hiring a draughtsman probably won't be necessary; and you will need to submit copies to the 'responsible authorities' (fire, police and so on) as stipulated by the licensing authority. Just as important as correctly observing the formalities is to consult as widely as possible in advance with neighbours (the term 'interested parties' includes schools, hospitals and businesses as well as residents). If you do your groundwork thoroughly the application you finally submit should be rubber-stamped.

As with planning, the key to reaching this happy outcome is to work closely with the council licensing officers handling your application: to be open with them and not to regard them as jobsworths to be bamboozled or placated or both. If treated with respect they can be – and indeed most of them want to be – extremely helpful, and can give you the advice that makes sure your application succeeds. They can suggest practical ways in which the four licensing policy objectives can be met (particularly with regard to supervision), which you may not have thought of. They will give you many invaluable tips, such as how to present the general description of the premises and the more detailed operating schedule as flexibly as possible, so you don't have to

> ### Pavement licences
>
> Permission to place tables, chairs and other temporary furniture (including, strictly speaking, your A-board) out on the public pavement is not included in your premises licence from the local council but requires a separate permit from the county council in its capacity as the highway authority. You can apply online but you will need to include a site-plan and a copy of your Public Liability Insurance certificate. There will also be a fee that varies from county to county.

keep varying your licence whenever you want to try something new. They will have issues of their own to raise, too: you might, for instance, be in or near an area where public drinking is prohibited, and they may ask what steps you propose to stop customers from drinking in the street (you may have to undertake to hire door staff at peak times). And each licensing authority will have its own policy regarding, for instance, disability access that the licensing officer can make you aware of and help you to fulfil. Once the licence is granted, that's the end of the process. Under the old system, pubs had to renew their licences every year and the public were allowed to object. Not now: all you have to do is pay a renewal fee.

In one sense the new procedure is a headache for licensees. Getting a new licence, or having an existing one varied, is far more costly and time-consuming than it used to be. But you only have to jump through the hoops once; and when that's done you're on a much more secure footing than you were. If you respect the terms of your licence it's hard for anyone else to get it reviewed or revoked (although the Act does give the police powers to close troublesome pubs on the spot). You've filed your flight-plan in fine detail, so to

Case study
Room with a Brew

As at the Mold Alehouse, planning and licensing both went smoothly when Nottingham's Scribbler's Ales opened its first micropub, Room with a Brew, in Derby Road just outside the city centre in February 2016. The bar was intended to be the first in a chain of three or four, which is the limit that the brewery in nearby Stapleford could supply without expansion. The brewery, owned by partners Rich Nettleton and Steve Mayes, retained specialist solicitor Shakespeare's to smooth the planning and licensing path, and it can only have helped that the city council owned the shop premises and was anxious to start getting some rent from it.

Room with a Brew was well received among hard-core beer-lovers in the city but being located in an up-and-coming part of Nottingham helped to bring in a more general clientele. It wasn't long before Scribbler's was on the hunt for its second site, and found it in a former sports shop in the suburb of West Bridgford. But things didn't go so well this time. Having had one painless experience, the partners thought they wouldn't need Shakespeare's services this time and could handle the process themselves. Unfortunately they were up against planning officers who didn't appear to know the law, and without a heavyweight professional advisor they were soon floundering.

In its consultation with residents, the brewery stressed that the bar would be small, would have no music or other entertainment and would close earlier than most pubs. "Despite that we had 16 objections, which the planning officers accepted as valid even though we had given all the necessary assurances," says Steve. "A handful of local people didn't understand the micropub concept and the council's officers sided with them, even though we got just as many letters of support."

Worse than that, the council officers seemed to put undue weight on the number of objections, which shouldn't be considered if the objections don't have valid planning grounds. And then came the last straw. "These planning officers said that Abbey Road was mainly an area of shops that closed at 6.00 pm, and if we promised to close at 8.00 pm they'd recommend granting permission," says Steve. "Of course we couldn't agree to that and anyway, it shouldn't be the planning officers' concern. Opening and closing times are for the licensing officers to agree. If we'd had specialist solicitors they could have put the officers straight. But we couldn't make any headway at all."

At this point the partners had three options: accept the unlawful planning condition and then simply ignore it, a path fraught with peril; appeal, a path fraught with uncertainty and anxiety; or just walk away. Which is what they did. "It's not as if Nottingham doesn't have plenty more empty shops," says Steve. At the time of writing Scribbler's had agreed terms on the lease of a former beauty salon and nail bar in Gedling, slightly further out into Nottinghamshire, and was hoping for a somewhat more straightforward planning and licensing process than they experienced in West Bridgford.

speak, and all concerned have had their say. Everything has been openly negotiated, and as long as you stick to the terms the council has approved, nobody (in theory) can complain.

Review and revocation

Nevertheless, you might still be accused of departing from the conditions of your licence. In this event Section 51 allows an 'interested party' (i.e. a disaffected neighbour) or a 'responsible authority' (i.e. the police or council officers) to ask the licensing committee to review all or part of your premises licence. The committee doesn't have to accede to such a request, for example if it isn't based on your fulfilment or otherwise of the licensing objectives; if it concerns a matter that has already been raised and resolved; or if the committee considers the application frivolous or vexatious, it won't.

If, however, the councillors feel that the matter needs to be dealt with they will give all parties sufficient time to marshal their arguments and evidence and will then conduct a hearing at which you and your accuser(s) will be able to put your respective cases. If the committee finds against you it can modify the conditions of your licence, such as remove one or more licensable activities from your licence; order you to appoint a better DPS (a trifle difficult if you're your own DPS!); suspend your licence for up to three months; or revoke it altogether. In practice, the more severe outcomes rarely arise from reviews at this level. Nine times out of 10 the dispute is going to be over noise, and the committee is going to make you turn off the amplifiers at 10 instead of 11 or might even stop you from having live music at all. In either case, you have the right of appeal.

More serious breaches will be dealt with by a summary review under Section 53. This class of action requires a certificate made out by a police Superintendant stating that

Planning and licensing

your pub is a hotbed of serious crime and/or public disorder. In this case the council can and probably will close you down within 48 hours. It must hold a hearing within 28 days and can apply the same range of sanctions as in the case of a Section 51 review. If you appeal, the sanction won't be applied until after the appeal is held.

Nobody picks up this book intending to incur the risk of a Section 53 review by condoning the activities of drug dealers or receivers of stolen goods, but it's not unknown for a licensee to lose control over a coterie of intimidating or violent customers, and you can easily find matters slipping away from you if you don't stamp it out fast. In the bad old pre-2003 Licensing Act days, many licensees were reluctant to report criminal activity in their pubs, not just because they were afraid of criminal repercussions but because they were afraid of the police as well, believing it would count against them at the Brewster Sessions (a meeting of magistrates to decide on and issue licences). Fortunately we don't have Brewster Sessions any more, and the police are likely to be very disappointed indeed if they find you, an upstanding citizen in a position of quite some social responsibility, withholding potentially valuable intelligence. So if in doubt, talk to the police. Some of them are really quite nice.

03

Legal matters

Recorded and broadcast music	56
Smoking	64
Sanitary facilities	68
Access and equality	69
Minors	76
Door supervisors and security	77

Case Studies

Beerhouse, Market Harborough	66
Kipps' Alehouse, Folkestone	74

You might think that the preceding chapters had placed a heavy enough burden of responsibility on your slender shoulders. Wrong! The licensed trade is among the most heavily regulated in the country, so here are some more burdens for you to bear, as well as the answers to some of the many legal questions that crop up from time to time.

Recorded and broadcast music

It's unthinkable, it sometimes seems, that we should be allowed out in public without being accompanied by music of some sort. But it comes as a shock to some and an affront to others that background music isn't free; that music is the intellectual property and indeed the livelihood of the musicians who compose and perform it; that anyone who plays it in public whether recorded, broadcast or live has to pay for it; and that the means exist to make sure that they do.

Regardless of this, music in various forms is an invaluable aid to your marketing: your choice of soundtrack is an assertion of your identity and hence of the identity of your clientele. Unchallenging classics such as the Four Seasons or the Pastoral Symphony playing gently in the background create an upmarket ambience that is reflected in the prices you can charge. Guitar music is a must for a tapas bar, but it doesn't have to be all flamenco – classical guitar or even a bit of gypsy jazz makes for a more sophisticated atmosphere and hopefully a more affluent set of regulars. A cocktail lounge that retreats some distance from contemporary R&B and other current chart genres to more retro jazz funk or jazz fusion will attract older patrons with fuller wallets. And you can easily set appropriate moods for different services throughout the day by changing the style and tempo of the music to suit.

Whatever you decide to play, if music makes money for you it's only right that the musicians should get their due.

The law that protects their rights, the Copyright, Designs and Patents Act 1988, requires the permission of the owner of the copyright of each and every song before it can be played in public whether it's via TV, radio, karaoke, a DJ set, a juke-box or a live act. The two bodies that enforce it are Phonographic Performance Ltd **www.ppluk.com**, which collects royalties on behalf of record companies and the musicians playing on each piece of recorded or broadcast music, and PRS for Music **www.prsformusic.com**, a joint agency of the Performing Right Society and the Mechanical Copyright Protection Society, which acts for composers and songwriters. How much you pay for your licences depends broadly, in the case of PPL, on the size of your premises and starts at £133 a year. PRS for Music's charging structure is rather more complicated but even at the top end it isn't enough to break the bank; PRS for Music has a calculator on its website. Inspectors from the two bodies are likely to call unannounced, and if they find you playing music without a licence they will demand your outstanding fees and their costs. If you refuse to pay they can sue, and the court will slap an injunction on you preventing you from playing any music until you've paid the back fees, inspector's costs and legal costs.

Live entertainment

Given the size of your bar, live bands probably don't form part of your business plan. You'd be astonished by how much floor-space a drum kit takes up! But if you fancy the idea of perching a classical guitarist on a bar stool in a corner to serenade your customers and add a touch of class, or allowing a close-up magician to wander around irritating people, or giving novice stand-ups their moment of terror and stammering, there's nothing stopping you. Solo acts – specifically stand-ups, for some reason, but presumably other similar turns such as magicians and contortionists as well – were not considered as licensable under the 2003 Licensing Act anyway and therefore didn't need local authority permission or a specific mention on the premises licence. Folk dancers and religious concerts were similarly exempt. Since then we've had the 2012 Live Music Act, which allows amplified or unamplified music for an audience of up to 200 on licensed premises between the hours of 8.00 am and 11.00 pm without anybody's by-your-leave at all. This uncharacteristic manifestation of libertarianism also embraces 'making music' and dancing, which is taken to mean karaoke and DJ sets.

There are caveats, however. The 2012 Act allows local authorities to impose conditions in cases where the entertainment creates noise (see below) or other nuisance or is seen as attracting crime. For instance, if you put on the kind of DJ sets that tend to attract underage fans, drug users and drug dealers, you will almost certainly be required to hire door supervisors and possibly to install CCTV.

Noise

Noise and nuisance, not just from entertainment but from the smoking shelter too, is likely to be well up in the top 10 of your headaches, and one of the worst things about it being that you're always in the wrong. You're in the wrong with your paying customers if you keep trying to shush them; but you're even deeper in the wrong with your neighbours, environmental health inspectors, the licensing authority and ultimately the courts if you don't.

Common law backed up by case law and statutes including the Environmental Protection Act 1990 and the Noise Act 1996 as well as a slew of other statutes, regulations and directives both British and European (listed in awesome fullness of the UK Environmental Law Association website **www.environmentallaw.org.uk**, give residents the right to quiet enjoyment of their homes; and of the various people and enterprises who are the targets of all this law – airports, building sites, the DIY enthusiast next door – you, the licensee, are the easiest to slap down. Neighbours complain to the local environmental health department about the 10.00 pm hilarity your stand-up has succeeded in creating, or the volume of Deep Purple on your vintage jukebox. The EHOs will either check you out or instruct your neighbours on how to gather evidence for themselves. If there's sufficient proof that you're a nuisance you'll receive an advisory visit followed, if you don't co-operate with the advice, by an abatement order. You have 21 days to appeal and if that fails you can receive an unlimited fine. Worse than that, you've breached the terms of your licence, which could therefore be revoked completely or in part.

In practice if you work with your neighbours – who, after all, are only trying to get some sleep – and with the environmental health department you can agree measures – some physical such as installing acoustic cladding, some procedural such as shutting the music down at 10.30 pm – that will hopefully satisfy all parties. Very often, though, when friendly agreements have been reached and 'Smoke on the Water' at 120 decibels is cool with everybody until 10 o'clock, one of your neighbours will sell their house to a newcomer for whom 'Smoke on the Water' at 120 decibels is not cool at any time of day or night. You may think, and many of your regulars will volubly protest, that people who don't like Deep Purple shouldn't buy houses next to bars where the punters do. You are entirely in the wrong, no ifs or buts. The newcomers' common law right to quiet enjoyment of their property is entirely unrelated to the compliance shown by the previous occupants. You were lucky that your former neighbours used their discretion in your favour, but their decision is not binding for their successors. Their reasons for choosing this particular property have no bearing on the case and aren't any of your business. All you can do is nod, smile, explain the situation amicably and try to reach an agreement with the newcomers (licensees have been known to offer to pay the neighbour's council tax, for example), while reflecting inwardly that actually you and your regulars agree with them and would demand the same rights if you found yourself in their situation.

Gaming

Ever since the 2005 Gambling Act took the shackles off internet betting, it has seemed that gaming in one form or another is all around us. Commercials for both high street and internet gaming, once a TV taboo, are prime time today, and betting shops are almost as common as charity shops. Despite dire predictions, there doesn't appear to have been an epidemic of dependency since the Act came into force, and perhaps the barrier between gambling and liquor that it sought to preserve might take some of the credit. In casinos proper the punters are perfectly at liberty to drink themselves stupid, handing their plastic and any vestige of inhibition to the croupier as they do so; as a bar owner you will find the law is rather more protective of your customers and stipulates that gaming should not be the main inducement for people to attend the premises.

This book sets out with the assumption that you intend to run a bar rather than a casino, and that if you'd wanted to run a casino that's what you'd be reading up on; nevertheless limited gaming provides a steady if ancillary income stream that you'd miss if it suddenly dried up. Events and promotions involving a certain amount of wagering can also be very popular lures, although the profit in these cases will almost all come through bar sales.

There are two forms of gaming that are pretty much taken for granted as being allowed in any pub or bar, one of which makes a profit for the house and the other of which doesn't. Any premises licensed for the sale of alcohol has an automatic entitlement to two machines graded either C (maximum stake £1, maximum payout £100) or D (mostly arcade-style games such as penny falls with small stakes and prizes). The entitlement can be removed by the licensing authority if it finds you're abusing it, especially if you allow minors to play class C machines (they are allowed to play the cheaper class Ds), which, of course, would breach one of the four licensing objectives. If you want more than two such machines there's a sometimes fairly tricky application to the licensing authority involved. The machines may only be sold or leased to you by a supplier licensed by the Gambling Commission: there's a register on its website **www.gamblingcommission.gov.uk**.

Unlicensed suppliers are by definition criminals, and doing business with them puts both your licences at risk. On class C machines you must also display signs advising that under-18s aren't allowed to use them and giving contact details for Gambling Support. One final point about machines is that you have to pay Machine Gaming Duty on them. For standard machines, including class C, this is 20 per cent of turnover, but to compensate you get a VAT exemption of, yes, 20 per cent. However ridiculous this seems, you still have to register with HMRC and submit a separate return although, in another stroke of make-work genius, you can add it all to your existing HMRC account.

The second sort of wagering that is generally allowed is small-stakes betting on games of skill, including darts, pool, bar billiards, dominoes, cribbage and shove-ha'penny, that might well be popular in a micropub that seeks to recreate the traditional public bar. Nobody knows what a small stake is, exactly: ask your licensing authority and you will get whatever answer is correct for your licensing district! And for some reason none of the usual variants of skittles and bowls are generally included on the approved list of games customers can bet on, even though they're just as skilful as any of the others listed. Again, what's legal and what's not depends very much on your licensing authority but as a rule of thumb, side-bets between players won't attract anybody's wrath but larger-scale betting by spectators at league games and tournaments very well might.

That's not the end of betting regulations for bar owners. You may host poker tournaments (not quite so popular as they were when the Act was framed) but there are very strict regulations to understand and comply with. You can let customers bet on the gee-gees using their own mobile phones or other devices but you may not facilitate sports betting by passing bets yourself (which has been rendered obsolete by online betting anyway). You can hold charitable events that involve limited amounts of betting, but the house may not profit therefrom. For a very good outline of the regulations governing all aspects of gaming in pubs go to **www.gamblingcommission.gov.uk** and search for gaming machines. You are also well advised to discuss your ideas at an early stage with both your licensing officer and the local police to determine their attitude and, if they seem broadly favourable or at least not outright hostile, consult your solicitor.

Televised sport

Televised sport has been a popular attraction in pubs and bars ever since all-day opening made it viable back in 1988. It has proved a much greater draw than many people originally predicted, but there have been downs as well as ups, notably over the fees charged by the Big Two satellite/cable TV companies Sky Sport and BT Sport.

This is not the place to go into the whys and wherefores of their strange fee structures and enormous costs: suffice it to say that a big sports pub (the fee is partly based on rateable value, so size matters), can easily end up paying £2,500 a month for their entire packages along with the output of smaller channels that show boxing and other sports – which, if you're making a profit out of it, is immaterial. You do get a fantastic amount of top-flight sport for your money, true, but you've still got a big job on your hands. And, of course, you don't have to pay anything except your licence fee to show all the sports that terrestrial channels can scrape together. But even then, the necessary hardware and installation costs can set you back £1,000 per unit.

So if you decide to specialise in sports TV, what can you realistically expect to get back? According to one estimate (not an independent estimate, mind you) a mid-sized premises that makes a feature of its sports programmes and promotes them hard can make £80,000 a year in additional sales, which if actually achieved is £40,000 in additional GP less maybe £18–19,000 in fees. Not huge, then, but well worthwhile – especially if you like sports yourself! At an average two hours and 40 minutes per visit, sports fans stay twice as long as other drinkers but only spend £3 a head more at £18 (£22 for rugby fans, though!) compared to £15. To encourage them to spend more lay on table service, which also has the advantage of eliminating the half time rush. Keep churning out those low cost-high turnover bacon and sausage baps, too, and maybe bowls of chips. And to stop end-of-match drift, switch channels to another live-action match immediately after the final whistle rather than hang around for the post-mortem.

But there's a but. Dismiss it as snobbery if you like, but there are large swathes of the population to whom the words 'big screen TV' are not an enticement to venture in but a warning to stay away. And while specialisation and segmentation have undeniable commercial advantages in an expanding market when you need to distinguish yourself from your competitors, they can be disastrous in a shrinking one when you need to attract every customer you can get.

The answer is partly to promote your sports to every possible customer via every possible medium, but equally not to forget that you welcome and serve anybody and everybody. It's no good gaining £80,000 in annual sales if you lose £200,000! Maintain a sport-free area if you have the space, with a cracking selection of cask beers and some dinky little artisan gins. Do food that's basic but good quality. Offer coffee and cakes for shoppers. Have a dress code and very, very good door staff. Keep everything spotlessly clean and in excellent repair. Clear the tables frequently. Sport is a great traffic-builder, but it mustn't be allowed to create a feeling of exclusion.

Smoking

Smoking in all enclosed public places in England (except letting bedrooms) was banned under the 2006 Health Act, which came into force on 1 July 2007. It had already been banned in Welsh, Scottish, Northern Irish and JD Wetherspoons pubs. Despite or perhaps because of the prolonged and highly contentious campaign preceding its enactment, the ban was accepted. Only two publicans openly defied it: one of them lost his licence almost on the spot, while the second was prosecuted and fined, refused to pay his fine, and was jailed. At time of writing e-cigarettes and vaping are perfectly legal in pubs, but many if not most operators have banned the practice because of the nasty haze it creates.

Regarding smoking shelters, the law says that no more than 50 per cent of your shelter may be closed in – the roof and the windward side, effectively – which is straightforward enough unless your pub possesses a courtyard that is more or less enclosed already and where environmental health officers might hem and haw before deciding how much more you can close off.

By and large freestanding permanent shelters and fixed canopies and awnings need full planning permission (although you might get away with a Lawful Development

Certificate), whereas portable awnings, gazebos and retractable canopies don't, and neither do portable space-heaters (which, by the way, can be very expensive to run!). Any addition, even wall-mounted ashtrays, that affects the character and/or appearance of the street frontage will probably need consent, doubly so if you're in a Conservation Area; and doubly-doubly so if your bar is a listed building. Ask the council's development control or planning department and they will give you a good steer as to what they'll consider and what they won't.

Pubs are allowed to sell cigarettes and other tobacco products, although cigarette vending machines became illegal in October 2011. If you do sell tobacco products you can't display them: since 2015 small retailers have had to follow larger stores in concealing them either in a cabinet, which you probably won't want, or at the very least under the bar. If you do this you also have to display an A3 sign stating in letters at least 36mm high: 'It is illegal to sell tobacco products to anyone under the age of 18' (which, of course, effectively advertises the fact that you sell cigarettes).

Cigarettes may now only be sold in packets of 20 and rolling or pipe tobacco in quantities of 30g, although there is no minimum pack-size for cigars. All packets must be standard grey-green without corporate branding, and with bigger health warnings than in the past. Do not buy stock that doesn't conform rigidly, or from any source you are unsure of: the standard packaging will make it easier for counterfeiters and smugglers to produce illegal cigarettes and if you or your staff or any of your customers sell these products in your pub, or take orders and/or payment in your pub for later delivery, you risk a fine, a prison sentence and the loss of your personal and/or premises licences.

Case study
Beerhouse, Market Harborough

Live entertainment is a no-no probably for most if perhaps not for all shop conversions. For micropubs it's virtually an article of faith that no music should be allowed to interrupt the flow of conversation; for most other bars it's a more practical question of space. At the Beerhouse in Market Harborough, though, space isn't a problem. The former furniture shop is almost too big even to be called a micropub: its main room and two snugs can seat 30-40 and at a pinch, can accommodate the same number again standing. It even has room for an upright piano. And as it's located in a courtyard with only offices for neighbours, noise is not a problem.

"I suppose we're untypical in many ways, although in common with other micropubs we're primarily about the beer," says manager Ben Marlow-Booth. That's 12 hand-pumps, four keg taps and a wide range of bottled beers, and the pumps are on constant rotation without even a regular house beer. "It annoys some people who might want more of what they had last night and find it's gone," admits Ben. "But we used to have a house bitter until sales just started falling away, so we stopped."

Market Harborough is a busy town with plenty of competition both for beer and for entertainment, so the Beerhouse tries to be a little different in its choice of artiste. Not too many middle-aged rock gods belting out Rainbow covers – "we're not all that drum kit-friendly," says Ben – but acoustic solo and double acts and, rather than electric bands, electronic ones. "They take up less space," he says. Open mic nights are particularly popular, although too open a welcome to local talent doesn't always pay off. A pure improvisation slot was dropped when people unaccountably started staying away in droves, and Ben acknowledges: "You do have to be a bit careful who you book."

It's not all music at the Beerhouse, though. Pub quizzes of course; a book club; comedy nights; and vinyl nights when customers bring along their own vintage 45s for a trip down memory lane. (People bring their own food, too, and not only takeaways but picnics, cheeseboards and even full Sunday roasts! Ben supplies the crockery and cutlery free on the strict understanding that none of it matches.) No banging DJ sets, though: the Beerhouse has a strict over-18s policy.

In hard commercial terms Ben shares the conventional wisdom that live events don't necessarily bring many extra customers in, although there are a few faces he sees only on live music nights. However, they do encourage people to stay longer (you don't go home halfway through a stand-up's slot unless you want to be followed out by a torrent of sarcastic witticisms) and hence spend more in the pub. But perhaps the real value of the Beerhouse's ceaseless programme of entertainment is summed up by one customer review on its Facebook page: "It felt like I was part of a community at the Beerhouse. Lots of music, lots of beer and lots of merriment!"

> ### Alcohol Wholesaler Registration Scheme
>
> Since 1 April 2017, licensees have had a new duty to perform – albeit not a terribly onerous one – under the Alcohol Wholesaler Registration Scheme. Anyone who retails alcohol to the public will need to ensure that the wholesale suppliers they buy their stock from have been approved under the scheme by checking the wholesaler's Unique Registration Number against the HMRC online database. Retailers found to have bought their liquor from an unapproved wholesaler may be liable to a penalty or could even face criminal prosecution and have their stock seized.

Sanitary facilities

Running a small bar as you do, you can get away with a single WC and handwash basin. Here, though, since you ask, is the British Standards Institute's recommended provision of WCs, urinals and washbasins.

- WCs: two for up to 150 men plus one for every additional 200 men; two for up to 40 men if urinals are not provided. Two for up to 25 women plus one for every additional 25 women up to 200.
- Urinals: one for every 50 men up to 200.
- Washbasins: Men – One per WC, plus one per five urinals or part thereof. Women – one, plus one per two additional WCs or part thereof. (Micropubs can get away with a single WC for everybody.)

It isn't actually a statutory requirement for men and women to have separate facilities, but the day of the unisex loo is not yet with us because most licensing authorities require separate provision. An additional requirement, but one you would have worked out for yourself anyway right after your first blocked drain, is that the ladies' should have disposal facilities for sanitary towels and tampons.

As we have seen, there is a requirement for washbasins (although not for soap), which implies a need for hand-drying facilities. After many years of research and counter-research, paper towels win on almost every count. They're quicker; they're more effective; they don't spread bacteria; and they're more ecologically friendly. You do have to empty the bins and replenish the dispensers, which you don't with electric dryers; but then you should be checking and servicing the toilet(s) frequently anyway, so this is just an added incentive to do so.

The whole question of disability access, including disabled toilets, is discussed at length below, but a disabled toilet is also of immense value if you have much family trade and should therefore be briefly mentioned here. First, many elderly people or people with an injury such as a broken leg find a disabled loo with its high seat, grab-handles, lever taps and greater space much easier to use than a urinal or a standard cubicle. Second, it's the optimum place for the baby-changing table and wipe dispenser. Third: when dad has to take a young daughter to the loo, or mum has to take a young son, having a gender-neutral toilet available can spare blushes. Not essential, true, but nice. And there's nothing wrong with nice!

Access and equality

The term 'public house', dates back to the late 18th century when the old distinctions between beerhouse, tavern, coffeehouse and dram-shop were beginning to blur. It's a handy catchall but it's also deeply misleading: while your house is indeed open to the public, the public has no right to enter except on your sufferance. You have exactly the same common-law right as any other householder to deny entry at your discretion and without giving a reason, and exactly the same right as any other householder to escort a trespasser off your property by the shortest possible route, using reasonable force where necessary. More than that, though, you have a duty to refuse service to certain categories of customer – i.e. those who are already drunk and those who are under 18.

Common-law rights and duties, though, can be overridden by statute, and the licensee's absolute right to control entry and service on a whim has been modified by a long series of anti-discrimination Acts over many decades: ever since, just to remind ourselves why, the scandalous and intolerable 'no blacks, no Irish' days of the 1950s, 60s and beyond. The current legislation is enshrined in the 2010 Equality Act and brings together and supersedes all the legislation that went before it. It identifies a number of 'protected characteristics against which discrimination is illegal', these being:

- Age
- Disability
- Gender reassignment
- Marriage/civil partnership
- Pregnancy and maternity
- Race
- Religion or belief
- Sex
- Sexual orientation.

The Act's definition of discrimination is that person A discriminates against person B if, because of a protected characteristic, A treats B less favourably than A treats or would treat others. Remember the Christian B&B owners who refused a gay couple a double bed? That was about as obvious a breach of the Act as it's possible to imagine, as was the case of the Christian baker who refused to make a wedding cake for a gay couple.

When controversy arises, it's often to do with breastfeeding. Should you banish breastfeeding mothers to the ladies' loo? Should you set aside a more comfortable private space for them? Should you offer them a large napkin or a hand-towel with which to protect their modesty? Or should you ban it altogether? The answer is simple, plain and incontrovertible: all these options are illegal. Whatever you or your customers think of breastfeeding in public places (including pubs, restaurants, cinemas, etc.), you are obliged to permit it without restriction, restraint or harassment. Under the Act it's illegal to stop or try to stop any mother of a baby up to 26 weeks old from breastfeeding; it's illegal to attempt to force the mother into a private room (especially a toilet! Yuck!) to breastfeed; and it's equally illegal for any of your customers to remonstrate with or abuse or otherwise harass her or her companions. It makes no difference if she reveals a breast while feeding: trying to get her to cover up by offering a towel or napkin, for instance, is harassment for which you can be sued through the county court and have costs and damages awarded against you or, in Scotland, face criminal proceedings with a fine of up to £2,500 plus costs.

On the other hand, many if not most breastfeeding mothers don't actually want to breastfeed in public, so you should also be prepared to offer any or all of the above facilities if requested. A bit of diplomacy is called for, though. If you do offer a nursing mother specific breastfeeding facilities then you must make it crystal clear that it's only a suggestion and not a request, let alone a requirement. And if a prudish customer kicks off (and they can be quite voluble), you need to advise them firmly but tactfully of the terms of the 2010 Act, particularly as regards to harassment.

In other cases, however, the correct application of equality law is not so clear-cut. The most high profile of these ambiguous areas is what happens when a transgender customer needs to use the loo and another customer objects. If the transgender customer in question possesses a certificate issued under the 2004 Gender Reassignment Act then that's the end of it: the reassignment is legally valid. If not, the decision as to which toilet the customer should use is best left to the customer (and there is, whatever people may think, no law that says men can only use the gents and women the ladies). As trying to impose your own opinion could and probably would be interpreted by a court as discrimination and harassment, your safest course of action is to do your best to placate the objecting party and restore peace. If the objector refuses to be placated then – even if they are a regular and the transgender customer isn't – your best bet is to eject the objector. It's the transgender customer, after all, who has the protected status, so when in doubt, protect. Hopefully this will never happen to you, but conflicts of this kind are on the increase; until there is a conclusive test-case, err on the side of inclusivity and acceptance and you can't go wrong.

Where the Equality Act will probably most concern you is in the arena of employment law. Everybody surely knows by now that advertising for a barmaid is a short-cut to the magistrates' court; but beyond that employment law is far too large a subject to be covered by this book and warrants a guide all of its own. You can download a free one at **www.employmentlaws.co.uk**, which also links you to Lawrite, a legal advice service you can subscribe to. However, you can get a very similar advice service for less as part of your membership of the Federation of Small Businesses.

There is, however, one aspect of discrimination and equality of which you can and should take full advantage, and that's disability access. The Equality Act recognises that many pubs are historic buildings that simply can't be adequately adapted for wheelchair users, especially in cases where the toilets are either upstairs or in basements, and therefore doesn't attempt to make such adaptations mandatory. Many planning and licensing authorities, however, will insist on disability access including disabled toilets in new applications or in alterations to premises that might make such provision feasible; and there are sound business reasons why you should design as much access as you can into whatever plans you are making. The obvious one is that there are about 3.6 million people in receipt of disability benefits in the UK, with a combined leisure spend of £2 billion. That's not actually a great deal because benefits are so miserly; but people with disabilities are great traffic-builders. They almost never seem to go out alone (a generalisation, but it seems to be true), which turns the 3.6 million into at least 7.2 million; and if they're going out as part of a group, the whole group will be pretty much obliged to select the pub that caters best to the particular needs of their friend. They also tend to return again and again to places that prove by deed that their custom is welcome.

We noted above that other categories of customer can benefit from a disabled toilet as well as the disabled themselves. Going back to our earlier theme, transgender customers might also feel more comfortable and relaxed using the disabled toilet, although it would be a mistake to try to direct them to do so. A disabled toilet is therefore an invaluable cash-generating asset that will amply repay its cost in very little time. As a fairly small bar you might only need to provide a single WC. If so, try to make it a disabled facility. A raised seat with support bars costs around £100 and can be installed in minutes; elbow-operated lever taps take some installing but still only cost around £80 (all these prices are taken from an online plumber's catalogue, **www.victorianplumbing.co.uk**, selected at random from a choice of hundreds). For more information visit **www.visitbritain.org/providing-access-all**: it's almost overloaded with advice and guidance on how to adapt your pub to make it disability-friendly.

Being disability-friendly isn't just about physical adaptations and equipment: it's equally important to train your staff to be just that – friendly. Not patronising or

Case study
Kipps' Alehouse, Folkestone

Access is a problem common to many if not most bars whether micropubs, cocktail bars, tapas bars or café bars, for no better reason than size. Wheelchairs need broad aisles between tables, and an adapted WC is more than twice the width of a standard cubicle. And to anyone in the hospitality industry, access means more than just making way for wheelchair users. No one knows that better than Andrew Pook, for the proprietor of Kipps' Alehouse in Folkestone is also a consultant in disability and housing.

At Kipps', he's widened and adapted the single cubicle so it now doubles as a ladies and a disabled WC (there's a separate gents), he's allowed for broader gangways between seating and he's changed all the lighting to non-flickering high-lumen LED, which is a help to people with sight impairments. "We're fortunate in that Kipps' was previously a restaurant, so we've got a bit more space and rather larger toilets than most micropubs," he says. "We also have a front door that's six-feet wide, which is ideal for wheelchair users."

Kipps' also welcomes children and dogs. Standing in the heart of Folkestone's picturesque cobbled old town, now dubbed the Creative Quarter and a popular tourist spot, Andrew could hardly turn his back on the family trade; and the area is also popular with dog walkers, many of them elderly. "Micropubs are especially popular with the more elderly customers because there are no distractions and not so much noise," says Andrew. "Having adapted facilities and welcoming dogs makes the bar much more inviting and comfortable for them. Children can be more of a problem, though, especially toddlers. Any pub, however clean and well-maintained it is, will present hazards for children and the licensee has to make sure that parents keep them close and under control. On occasion I have had to stress that while a child is on my premises I'm responsible for its wellbeing, which can lead to conflict with the parents. But on the whole we're very active in welcoming families because we're part of the Creative Quarter."

At the time of writing Andrew was on the lookout for a second branch and had inspected more than 40 empty shops. "I know that some commercial premises don't have to meet all the access requirements for customers with disabilities, but I've been shocked at how little provision there is in the premises I've visited," he says. "The ageing population is a ticking time-bomb for high street businesses. Trade is hard enough as it is, and if they don't take their responsibilities to the elderly and people with disabilities a lot more seriously, eventually they won't be able to trade at all."

overbearing, but straightforward and relaxed, with none of the awkwardness and embarrassment that seems to overcome many people. A signer or two wouldn't come amiss, either.

Minors

Any book of this sort is going to be so liberally sprinkled with warnings against serving alcohol to minors that further information might seem hardly necessary. Not so. There's a fair bit of law on the subject, which you ought to at least be familiar with even if your bar is not exactly family-friendly. So here it all is (mostly).

The 2003 Licensing Act allowed under-16s accompanied by an adult (i.e. aged over 18) into all parts of licensed premises and swept away the old law prohibiting them from bar areas, which had been an unenforced and unenforceable dead letter for more than a decade. It maintains all the same prohibitions against under-18s buying, being bought or drinking alcohol on licensed premises that had been introduced 95 years earlier in the 1908 Children Act, but while it relaxed a lot of antique restrictions it also introduced a new one. Previously it had been arguably legal to buy an alcoholic drink (i.e. containing more than 0.5% ABV) for a child to consume in a part of the premises not exclusively or primarily concerned with the sale and consumption of alcohol, in particular the garden. The 2003 Act closed the loophole simply by changing the wording to 'relevant premises'.

The standard defence when charged with breaches of these laws – that no reasonable person could have suspected, on the basis of personal appearance, that the offender was under 18 – was also maintained, but in a significantly modified form: to the old 'but she looked 18' defence it added the proviso that the person serving the drink had asked for and been shown credible proof of age.

The law now allows children under 16 accompanied by adults over 18 to be on licensed premises between 5.00 am and midnight, although in practice few licensees would let them stay so late unless there were exceptional circumstances. It has become accepted practice to ask parents with younger children to leave by 8.00 or 9.00 pm, but it's not stated in the Act. However one of the four licensing objectives is the protection of children from harm, and the council's licensing committee or liquor control board might very well consider a curfew to be evidence of your commitment to that objective.

The 2003 Act, incidentally, did preserve another old and little-known loophole which many at the time thought might be done away with. You are and always have been allowed to sell beer, cider and wine to 16- and 17-year-olds who are accompanied by an adult and are eating a substantial table meal – steak, chips and mushrooms, for example, eaten with a knife and fork, but not a hand-held steak sandwich. However, this is counterbalanced by your responsibility not to sell alcohol to people who are or who appear to be drunk: a single pint of farmhouse cider at 6% or 7% ABV would probably be enough (or more than enough) for most 16- and 17-year-olds!

Door supervisors and security

Depending mainly on the location of your pub, your premises licence may require you to engage a specified number of door staff at specified times. A warning: your cousin Alan and his mates from the rugby club might be pretty intimidating geezers who know how to handle themselves in a ruck, but that does not qualify them to act as doormen. In 2007, following the infiltration of many door security agencies by violent organised criminal gangs, especially drug dealers and extortionists, the industry was thoroughly regulated and all security personnel must now be trained, licensed and registered by the Security Industry Authority. If your premises licence requires you to hire door staff you will find details of fully compliant operatives and agencies listed on **www.sia.homeoffice.gov.uk**. Try to find an agency that deploys women as well as men: for reasons we can argue about all night they seem to be more successful at calming tensions and preventing fights. As a well-run pub, though, you're less likely than a club to attract trouble: your door staff will probably find themselves busiest keeping the noise from the smoking shelter down and preventing customers from taking glasses off the premises. Expect to pay £10–£15 an hour, depending on where you are and what level of service you require.

It's perfectly possible and indeed desirable to get SIA training for yourself and perhaps a key member of staff. The 45-hour courses are typically taught over two weekends (although they can be taken online) and involves three exams, and cost £150–£250. Course providers are listed on the SIA website. The advantages, especially in a busy pub with a largely younger clientele, are obvious. You'll know how to spot potential flare-ups and quell them before things get out of hand. You'll learn how to spot the signs of drug use, drug dealing and trafficking in stolen goods. You'll put yourself in a good light with the police and licensing authorities. And best of all, getting SIA training for yourself and some staff (and maybe even Alan and his mates from the rugby club!) might well fulfil any requirement in your licence for door supervisors, which will save you an awful lot of money.

For additional security you might also want to consider installing CCTV, which many licensing authorities used to make mandatory until a code of practice limiting their power to do so was introduced in 2012. The reason why the code was introduced was that publicans and many of their customers objected that CCTV was not only expensive and intrusive but also very often ineffective, so do think very carefully about the benefits and the risks before you make any spending decisions. If you're in a location that's vulnerable to burglary – suburban, deserted at night, lots of nooks and crannies to hide in – CCTV is a proven deterrent, especially when combined with security lighting. But – and there are a lot of buts – it has to be expensive, with very high resolution, or all it will capture is blurs. It doesn't seem to have the same deterrent effect in town centres when the youths causing the disturbances are often too drunk to care. There are also privacy issues relating to indoor CCTV, especially in toilets where they're least acceptable but (if your pub has a drug problem) most required. You might site a camera to see whether more than one person at a time is entering a cubicle, but not one that will show what they get up to once they're in there! And there are potentially very serious data protection issues depending on where the cameras are pointed and how the images they record are stored. If you're considering CCTV, get advice from a police crime prevention officer first; and when getting quotes try to establish how well the installers you talk to understand the legal ramifications. The Health and Safety Executive has excellent guidance covering all CCTV-related issues at **www.hse.gov.uk/violence/toolkit**.

Pets

Some people don't like dogs in pubs; others think they ought to be part of the furniture. If you want to exploit the family trade you're probably better off siding with the latter.

First things first: there is no legal reason why you shouldn't have dogs anywhere on the premises except in the kitchen. The legislation relating to dogs in food premises is contained in EU Regulation 852/2004, which states:

'Adequate procedures are to be in place to prevent domestic animals from having access to places where food is prepared, handled or stored (or, where the competent authority permits, to prevent such access from resulting in contamination).'

The regulations do not prohibit the presence of dogs in catering establishments such as pubs, restaurants and takeaways, which remains at the discretion of the proprietor. However, all food businesses are responsible for ensuring that their own food safety management procedures identify and control risks to food hygiene. The local Environmental Health Department should be satisfied that the business has adequate controls in place to prevent the risk of contamination. (Allowing guide or other assistance dogs into food premises is covered by the requirements of the Disability and Discrimination Act 1995.) There is therefore no restriction preventing dogs from being in areas where food is served.

If you're going to let dogs into your pub, though, make it crystal clear that it's up to their owners to keep them under control and that you're the one who defines what 'control' means. A single customer with a badly behaved dog – not necessarily a vicious one, but one that won't settle, that jumps up or begs at other people's tables etc. – can drive away regulars, so it's up to you to be diplomatic but firm and bar badly behaved dogs and their owners. Conversely, if you want to make the most of being dog friendly, be really dog friendly. A frequently replenished drinking bowl. A big bag of dog nibbles behind the bar. A few bits of old rope or other dog toys in the garden. An emergency supply of poo-bags. And most important of all a friendly smile, a stroke or a pat and a scratch behind the ears. Dog people love people who love their dogs, and if you're really dog friendly rather than just tolerant, dog owners and their wallets will be back.

The Craft Distillers' Handbook

A practical guide to the making and marketing of spirits

Ted Bruning

"This is a brilliant book for those seeking to know what running a distillery entails and how to get started"

Alex Davies, Head Distiller, Kyoto Distillery, Japan

- Microdistilling has never been more popular. The number of gin distilleries alone, opening in the UK in 2016, was 45 with gin sales now reaching £1 billion.
- A very practical guide with 10 case studies of those who have started their own distilleries.
- Get inside information on developing the necessary skills, calculating the finances and finding the right premises.
- Find out what equipment you'll need, where to get it – and how much you would pay!
- Formulate and market your own brand of top-quality spirits and liqueurs.
- **£12.95 plus postage and packing**

www.posthousepublishing.com

04

Beer and cider

Know your beers	84
Cask versus keg	85
Real ale formats	88
Cellar skills	90
Keg, smooth and craft	97
Bottles and cans	99
NLA beers	101
Cider	105
Guest ales and promotions	107

Case Studies
Just Beer, Newark	*94*
The Rake, Southwark, London	*108*

Beer is what pubs are all about, or so many believe, and perhaps they're right: after all, a pub with no beer is the subject of song. In fact, one of the defining characteristics of a micropub, according to the Micropub and Microbrewery Association, is its commitment to real ale. Indeed many of its members, as the organisation's name suggests, brew their own beer and by taking advantage of small brewery relief enjoy a 50 per cent duty discount and become even more profitable. But while beer is one of the things that define a pub, few today survive on beer sales alone; and those that do tend not to be old-fashioned locals but specialist bars for hard-core enthusiasts.

Know your beers

This might be taken as the ideal opportunity to insert a long and erudite gazetteer of beer styles (of which there are now reputed to be more than 150), complete with scholastic exegeses on the actual difference between stout and porter, the absurdity of the very notion of black IPA, whether the term 'mild' derives from a low hop-rate or some other quality, and how long lager should be lagered before it becomes lager. But it's such a huge topic that it merits a book to itself – and in fact that book that has already been written many, many times by many, many authors. Read them by all means, but do so for pleasure. For the shape and nature of the industry and its products are changing so fast that any beer book you read will be out of date by the time it reaches you; and if you're already at the point where you've decided to open a bar whose main attraction is going to be its beers, you probably already know all that you need to know about the subject anyway. A sharp eye on the trade press, a keen ear on your customers' conversations and regular attendance at the trade sessions of beer festivals are the best ways of keeping up to date.

For you can't be a walking encyclopaedia of beer: there's

simply too much to know. Truth be told, even as someone who depends on beer for a living you really only need three things: a good grasp of the different styles so you can stock a balanced range without duplication; a deep understanding of what your clientele expects; and the ability to recognise faults in the beer even if you're not really a beer drinker yourself. You don't have to be a connoisseur to know when something's not right.

Cask versus keg

Knowing your beer styles is rewarding in itself and will help your marketing enormously. But the ferocious zealotry, fanatical passion and superheated debates that have surrounded beer and brewing for the past half century have had little to do with styles. The dire state of the nation's ale in the early 1970s sparked an explosion that saw the number of small independent breweries soar from a dozen or so to nearly 2,000 at the time of writing, triggering a cultural tsunami that laid low six of the country's largest, richest and most powerful corporations and changing the structure of the whole hospitality industry. And it all started as an argument not about the beer itself, but about how it ought to be dispensed.

Keg beer was first produced in the 1930s as a means of prolonging shelf life by processing draught beers exactly as breweries already processed their bottled beers. Filtered, pasteurised, carbonated and filled into airtight containers, bottled beer was virtually imperishable. Any air that might have oxidised the beer was (hopefully) excluded by efficient modern bottling, and any spoilage organisms – whether fungal or bacterial – were poisoned by a lethal combination of alcohol, hop-derived acids and carbonation. The extension of bottling technology to draught beer was pioneered in Germany and in pre-war Britain it enabled small weekend-only accounts like the East Sheen Lawn Tennis Club (supposedly Britain's first retailer of keg ale) to stock a draught ale that wouldn't go bad before it could all be sold. But that wasn't really the point.

To fulfil its true destiny the new technology had to wait until after the war when enough steel became available to allow the mass-production of metal kegs (Guinness used its first metal keg in 1946 and its last wooden one in 1963). The aim wasn't to provide sports clubs with draught beer on the two days a week when their bars were open, though – it was to allow rapidly growing breweries to service huge and far-flung tied estates with brewery-conditioned beers that would remain stable from leaving Flower's at Stratford-on-Avon or Green's at Luton (two early advocates) until arriving at their most distant tied house. Upon arrival, all the beer in the keg would be saleable, unlike cask ale of which 10per cent might easily have to be poured away.

But how did this technological stride provoke such a widespread revolt? After all, the same process was being adopted across Europe, and as long as the liquid in the keg was all right, Dutch, Belgian and German connoisseurs were scarcely even disgruntled. But British brewers took things a step too far. They quickly realised that pasteurisation and the high dosage of CO_2 involved in kegging between them killed any chance of spoilage while the packaging prevented oxidisation. This rendered both the alcohol (the dutiable and therefore expensive fraction of the liquid) and the hops (also expensive) pretty much redundant, so they started making weaker and weaker and fizzier and fizzier beer, serving it well-chilled to mask the lack of hop flavour. European breweries largely eschewed these practices, but in Britain pasteurisation and substandard beers such as Watney's notoriously weak Starlight were foisted on an unhappy public. The Campaign for Real Ale, which was founded in 1972, was such an instant success because it struck a chord that resonated with almost every adult male in Britain.

The expression 'real ale' is a linguistic paradox. Everyone who knows their beer understands, or claims to understand, exactly what it means, and yet it means nothing. All ale is real: it is all made by mashing ground malted barley in hot water, boiling the resulting syrup with hops and then fermenting it. Keg beer is not synthetic, it is merely processed. Brewers themselves prefer the expressions 'cask-conditioned', meaning that the beer hasn't quite finished fermenting when it is racked, and 'brewery-conditioned', meaning that it has. And before CAMRA came along there was no notion that some beer was real and some wasn't. Even the four Manchester journalists who founded CAMRA didn't have the idea to start with. At first they called their brainchild the Campaign for the Revitalisation of Ale: the name hardly tripped off the tongue and was soon changed. But if 'real ale' started life not as a definition but as a slogan, it quickly acquired a very strict meaning: unpasteurised and unfiltered beer, packaged with enough live yeast to keep it working gently and served without extraneous gas. None of this makes it 'real'; it might just as well have been called fresh beer or living beer, as either would have been more accurate. But 'real ale' quickly turned out to have high public recognition, and therefore the name stuck.

However made-up the terminology may be, though, the liquids thus described are different and need different handling. Keg beer is what it is: it's almost inert and will keep almost forever provided the ambient temperature is moderate and stable. Learn how to connect the keg, the pipes and the CO_2 canister and set the gas correctly, keep the lines clean, serve the beer at the right temperature, tilt the glass and pour steadily… and that's pretty much it. Every customer will get just what they ask for and just as they want it, and you can't argue with that. Real ale is a far more sensitive beast.

Real ale formats

Real ale usually comes in nine-gallon metal (or, increasingly, heavy-duty plastic) casks or firkins. Full-sized 36-gallon brewers' barrels are now almost obsolete and the word is only used as the industry's standard unit of account. Even kilderkins or half-barrels are comparatively rare these days. The firkin reigns supreme because even in the bigger accounts beer generally sells more slowly than it used to and is at risk of going off if sold from a larger container; because it allows specialist alehouses to stock a greater variety; and because at 50kg filled weight it's (comparatively!) easy to handle.

Once in the cellar and lying safely on their convex sides on their racks or stillages the casks are normally connected to a beer-line, which is connected in turn to a vacuum-pump mounted on the bar-counter and actuated by the familiar hand-pump. Alternatively the beer can be poured direct from tap to glass. This latter method, called gravity dispense, is very common in micropubs that often don't have cellars or even separate stillrooms. It has other advantages than mere space saving, though, the main one being that it vastly reduces waste as there are no lines from which leftover beer has to be run off. It also makes the beer hoppier, since the turbulence caused by the action of the beer pump drives off some of the aromatic hop volatiles, which then dissipate as the beer is poured. Gravity is the usual method of dispense at beer festivals; indeed the cooling jackets you now see everywhere were actually designed for use at festivals.

The drawback is that the beer pours without much head and to a northerner it appears flat. It's an illusion: southern and gravity-poured pints may come without a head, but that's because all their CO_2 is still dissolved in the body of the beer, whereas the northern pint's inch-deep head is composed jointly of the air whipped into it and the CO_2 knocked out of it by the agitated pour – so technically a pint with a big foaming head is flatter than a pint with a few mournful bubbles collected on the top. But you can't tell a Tyke that, and if you happen to be opening a bar north of the Trent you might have some difficulty explaining that actually your ale is NOT flat. Under these circumstances, and even if you have no cellar but pour your ale direct from casks mounted where the public can see them, you might still feel it wise to go through the charade of connecting them to a beer-line and hand-pump. In which case be sure to use a swan-neck – an elongated curved spout shaped like a swan's neck – with a sparkler or removable perforated plate screwed on to the end of the spout. If a customer with a softie southern accent asks you to remove the sparkler, always do so without question. You may secretly sneer at and even despise the southerner with his penchant for flat beer, but you don't despise his money and it costs nothing to be obliging even to someone from Surrey.

Before leaving the topic of formats, there is one traditional cask size that's very handy for slower-moving beers, especially the stronger winter ales, and that's the 36-pint pin. Metal pins are very rare these days because they cost almost as much as firkins but are both desirable and easy to steal. Instead, brewers have turned to the disposable bag-in-boxes universally known as polypins. These now-familiar recyclable plastic cubes are lightweight, tough, cheap and, being one-way only, convenient. They can prolong the beer's life from four days to four weeks, and are ideal for trying beers you're not certain of, for slow-selling seasonal or extra-strong specials and for festivals and outside bars. The only doubt that might be raised is whether their contents are strictly 'real', since the beer is often filtered to stop the secondary fermentation that unchecked might blow the polypin. This also means the beer is already bright and doesn't need time to clear, hence the poly's suitability for festivals and outside bars. But this one niggle aside, they are now broadly accepted within the real ale community.

A modern variant on the bag-in-box is the KeyKeg, which isn't a keg at all. The box isn't actually a box, either: it's a rigid airtight cylinder of 10, 20 or 30 litres containing a collapsible plastic bag full of beer. Compressed air is pumped into the space between cylinder and bag, forcing the beer out without actually coming into contact with it, thereby preventing the beer from oxidising. The beer might be filtered in order to pour bright, but as long as it's not pasteurised as well it is still widely accepted as 'real' (although if it is pasteurised, the elimination of spoilage microorganisms will extend the beer's life yet further). After use the bag is stamped down flat, folded up and put into the recycling bin. KeyKeg is catching on fast with the trade because by extending shelf life it virtually eliminates waste and widens the range of ales the licensee can safely stock. It's light and therefore cheap to transport and easy to handle in the cellar; it's easy to change; the compressed air is cheaper and safer than CO_2 – and as it's one-way you don't have a car park stacked with unsightly empties.

Cellar skills

Many if not most micropubs and craft beer bars won't actually have a cellar but will keep their beer in a back room, either an old stockroom or even a former kitchen. Wherever you keep it, though, getting a pint of real ale from cask to customer in a drinkable state takes care, a degree of skill and above all dedication. And it starts and ends, pretty much, with hygiene.

Hygiene is important with cask beer as it is with food, because few dispense systems can be truly hermetically sealed and, since bugs simply adore sugary goo, there are endless opportunities for infection. Scrupulous hygiene – including taking an old toothbrush to every connector – is absolutely essential: not just frequent, regular and painstaking scrubbing with non-contaminant cleaning materials, but also annual repainting with a recommended mould-resistant paint. For a simple but complete step-by-step guide to cellarmanship Alex Hall's instructions cannot be bettered – visit **www.cask-ale.co.uk**. CAMRA also has an invaluable booklet on the subject, entitled simply Cellarmanship. But as a basic guide:

- Cellar or still-room temperature must be constant. The ambient temperature doesn't matter with keg beers, although a low temperature gives the flash cooler less work to do and saves money. For real ale the ambient cellar temperature should be 8–10°C for a service temperature of 10–12°C. Don't pull cask beer through a cold python or it will pour too cold, too flat and could even be chill-hazed.
- Give cask beer time to drop bright before you tap it – seven days if you can manage it, but three or four days at the very least. Once it's tapped, though, it has only another three or four days before oxidation sets in. Higher gravity beers keep their condition slightly longer, and there is also a simple device that gives real ale an extra day or two's life without breaking anyone's rules. The race spile is a one-way valve inserted into the spile hole and set to one bar – i.e. it will let the natural CO_2 generated by secondary fermentation build up in the headspace of the cask as the beer-level drops, and will vent automatically when the gas pressure in the cask reaches a single atmosphere. It also lets you off the last-thing-at-night (and often forgotten about) chore of hard-spiling all the casks.
- Another option for prolonging the life of the beer and maintaining its condition is more controversial. This is the cask breather or ventilator, which fills the headspace of the cask with CO_2 at one bar as the level of the beer sinks. The CO_2 performs the double purpose

of killing bacteria and other spoilage organisms and preventing the beer from oxidising; and at one bar the gas won't dissolve in the beer. If you use one of these, though, CAMRA won't list you in its Good Beer Guide.

- The cleaner the cellar the less chance there is of contamination, so keep everything – including walls, ceiling and cellar steps or ramp – clean all the time. Wash down the cellar door-flaps after every delivery. If the cellar is damp, watch carefully for mould and get rid of it before it builds up. Never use perfumed cleaning products or bleach: use an antibacterial agent or even line-cleaner.
- Flush each pipe with clean water whenever you change a barrel if you can, but clean all the pipes thoroughly every seven days at least. Although automatic systems only take 10 minutes rather than 45, a lot of publicans still prefer to clean their lines manually because it means they can inspect them as they clean. When you clean the pipes scrub the barrel connectors using a toothbrush and line-cleaner. Even the outsides of the beer lines have to be washed down. And before you tap a barrel, clean all around the spigot hole – some barrels are filthy when they come in.
- Carried out frequently, these routines should only take 15–20 minutes a day, with one morning a week devoted to the big wash-down. As with housework, the more often you do it, the less there is to do.
- Bar staff need to be just as scrupulous when serving the beer as the licensee is in the cellar. Clean the spouts regularly with a non-bleach antibacterial wipe, especially on swan necks, and never use the same glass twice. If someone's got a cold and you put the spout into the beer, the spout is contaminated and so is the

Cask Marque
www.cask-marque.co.uk

The simplest and most effective way to promote the quality of your real ale is to get an independent expert to endorse it, and the simplest and most effective way to do that is to join Cask Marque.

The heatwave of July 1997, when the temperature in some parts of the country topped $100^{0}C$, was a disaster for cask ale, which in those days was seldom distributed on refrigerated trucks or kept in temperature-controlled cellars. But it did give us Cask Marque, an organisation set up by some of the larger regional breweries to improve the quality of their flagship product by testing it at the point of sale and accrediting the best retailers. Heading the organisation was former Adnams managing director and one of the most respected men in the industry, Paul Nunny, still in the post after 20 years. But critical to its success was its credibility with the public, who must not be allowed to dismiss it as just another marketing gimmick. That rested on two factors: first, an objective test carried out twice a year of the beer's quality and measuring its appearance, aroma, flavour and temperature; and second, a cadre of highly experienced ex-brewers and quality control managers who travelled the country to administer the tests on unannounced visits. Another plank in the scheme's credibility was that publicans who wanted the accolade of a Cask Marque certificate to display on the doors of their pubs had to subscribe, so that no cynic could claim that it was just a brewery-financed stunt.

Today there are some 45 Cask Marque assessors covering sampling and scoring of ale at more than 10,000 pubs. Along with their certificates and associated merchandise, the pubs that pass the assessments are promoted on Cask Marque's website.

Case study
Just Beer, Newark

Real ale, keg beer, craft – there's a lot of very loose definitions in the world of beer and bars and, as with many folk idioms, they don't carry any intrinsic meaning: you either know or you don't. 'Micropub' is another such term. The word itself doesn't include any reference to beer but the founders of the Micropub and Microbrewery Association insist that a commitment to real ale is part of the definition, and as the public seems to have taken their insistence to heart, so be it.

You don't get much more committed than the Newark micropub pithily entitled 'Just Beer'. Of course you are greeted by eight hand-pumps, at least four of which are always on. Naturally there is always a traditional cider or perry in the cold room. It goes without saying that there's a chiller cabinet with a selection of Belgian and German bottled beers, as well as gluten-free and low-alcohol for those who want them. And you will be equally unsurprised by the lack of piped music, lager, wines and spirits, alcopops and cooked food. (Although those staples of the micropub table, locally made pork pies, good-quality cheese and proper pork scratchings, are all present and correct.) All this would bring a smile to the face of the father of the micropub, Martyn Hillier. But there's more.

The bar's address – Swan & Salmon Lane – identifies it as the former stables of the Swan and Salmon in Castle Gate, an 18th-century posting house that's still trading under a new name: the Riverside. And the Four Tapsters who founded and still run the place – Dunc, Merf, Phil and Stu, aka Duncan Neil, Paul Murphy, Phil Ayling and Stuart Clancy – are all former chairmen of Newark CAMRA, and the idea of starting a micropub came to Phil direct from Martyn Hillier himself – he describes Martyn's address to CAMRA's 2008 AGM as "a jaw-dropping moment".

A draughtsman by trade with more than 30 years' experience, Phil says: "I'd been unemployed for some time after getting my umpteenth redundancy cheque and I was pretty fed up with job-hunting when I heard Martyn speak and thought, 'this is what I want to do'. I'd worked at Newark CAMRA's beer festival for 17 years and I was pretty familiar with handling and serving real ale, so I thought I'd make my hobby my living."

The old stables had long been empty after a fruitful career as an art gallery and studio, and it took some restoring. New toilets had to be built from scratch, and although the building itself isn't listed the pub and its surroundings are, so the job required listed building consent. What came out of it was a long, narrow room with seating for 25 and standing room for another 10–15; the dimensions of the room mean that the more sociable regulars can congregate up at the bar end while the solitary pint-and-a-paper customers can enjoy a bit of peace and quiet at the other. It all made the conversion a lot more expensive than most micro pubs and something of a gamble, but it was all worth it. Newark's beer lovers took to the bar so quickly that it was in the black from day one. It helped that the Four Tapsters are so CAMRA-savvy that they could push all the right buttons: oversized lined glasses, at least one beer from a local brewery, traditional pub games (the shape of the room allows for a dartboard, too) and, despite its size, regular beer festivals with up to 17 ales on at a time. One coincides with the CAMRA event at the end of May, but the surprise hit is the event jointly staged by town-centre pubs in late January every year. "It started with us and two other pubs, so we called it the Beermuda Triangle Festival, and although there are seven pubs in it now the name seems to have stuck," says Phil. "Perhaps it's that time of year when people need cheering up but we get though 25 firkins every time, guaranteed."

On its seventh birthday, Just Beer announced that it had served more than 3,700 real ales, but by then an intruder had quietly crept into the bottle-chiller: canned craft beer. Sacrilege, surely? "I'll drink any good beer," says Phil. "In my view you can't beat cask but there are some stupendously good craft beers out there. The only thing I don't like about them is the price. But I was in the centre of Hull the other night and the traditional pubs were quiet while all the craft bars were rammed even at £7–£8 a pint."

Just Beer, apart from those cans, is sticking to its real ale guns, but Phil himself with other partners has already opened Beerheads craft beer bars in Retford and Grantham, with more planned for Nottingham, Lincoln and Melton Mowbray. Just Beer describes itself as 'an old-fashioned bar with modern attitudes'; and as Phil demonstrates, there's no conflict involved in having a foot in both camps.

next pint you pour. At the end of the night spray the spouts with antibacterial. And staff who slip out for a sly cigarette should always wash their hands before returning to service: hand to mouth to glass equals hand to cold/flu/herpes to glass.

Keg, smooth and craft

Real ale may make all the headlines, but it doesn't make all the sales. Far from it. Maybe the tide of keg ales has been ebbing since the 1990s, but most of the beer served in Britain is still filtered, pasteurised, carbonated and chilled. For lager makes up the bulk of beer sales, both draught and packaged, and it is therefore true to say that more than half of Britain's beer drinkers choose full-on fizzed-up ice-cold keg beer because that's how they like it.

There is another processing format that they might have turned to instead: smooth beer is processed like keg beer but is protected and propelled by low-pressure nitrogen, which unlike CO_2 doesn't dissolve in the beer. But smooth has only caught on as a format for draught ales, and is at its most popular in venues such as hotels and restaurants that want to carry a draught ale or two but feel that the old-style CO_2-driven keg is too downmarket. The delivery of smooth beer is very much closer to cask ale than keg is: lager drinkers, however, seem to prefer the full-on attack of CO_2 to the less aggressive nitrogen. There are no lagers whose usual format is smooth.

Then there's the newcomer. Craft, like 'real', is a term that in the context of beer has no inherent meaning. In the mid-1980s when today's Society of Independent Brewers was formed, its founders toyed with the name Craft Brewers' Association but dismissed it on the grounds that the word 'craft' implied amateurism, and that they didn't want to be taken for home brewers. The term re-emerged much more recently when a new generation of microbrewers, inspired by the example of small brewers in the USA, began producing keg beers that, they argued, would always reach the drinker in the condition they intended. There had already been a number of pioneers producing top-quality processed beers in Britain for a long time, all of them either foreign or influenced by foreign brewing practices. Alistair Hook, founder of Meantime Brewery, Greenwich, trained in Germany; the late Oliver Hughes of the Porterhouse Brewery, Covent Garden, was Irish; Jeff Rosenmeier of Lovibonds of Henley-on-Thames is American. Despite the undoubted quality of the beers they produced (and in Rosenmeier's case, still produce), they were rather sneered at by the ale-loving élite and their beers were not welcome at CAMRA festivals. But the US-inspired craft brewers who have emerged since are too numerous to be ignored and in most cases too inventive and too accomplished to be sneered at.

The word 'craft' was therefore taken up as a polite way of sidestepping the awkward truth that their beers were in fact straightforward keg; but of course nobody could hang a fixed definition on such a vague descriptor and before long any brewer of any size was describing every beer it brewed as 'craft'. Keg beers, whether they call themselves 'craft' or not, are still not always welcome at CAMRA festivals, but from your point of view as a retailer there is one solid and very positive upshot: keg beer is respectable again. Provided the beer is good and your customers are happy with it there is no fallout from stocking it. And there's a double whammy: not only do you get to sell all 11 gallons in an 11-gallon tub (50 litres, the standard size for kegs, gives away the format's Continental origins), you can get away with charging quite a hefty premium for it as well.

Finally, craft brewers really let their imaginations run wild and some of them know no limits in what they'll try brewing with. More traditionally-minded brewers are dismissed as 'twiggies' and if you want a beer that tastes of anything from chocolate to roses there's someone out there brewing it, so you get a constant stream of new and exciting beers on which you can make more money.

Bottles and cans

Originally, most bottled beers were no more than processed versions of the brewery's draught beers, brown being bottled mild, light being bottled bitter and so on. Because their quality was reliable they were more expensive than draught beers. Guinness was supplied in bulk from Dublin (and, after 1926 from Park Royal in West London) to regional and local brewers for bottling (a draught version wasn't generally available in the UK until after 1953), and because of its high price it was widely regarded as a treat. In pubs where the condition of the draught ale was particularly unreliable it was common to drink light and bitter or brown and mild: that way you could (in theory) guarantee reasonable quality at an affordable price. Bottled beers were also, of course, for taking home at a time when pubs were forced to close long before their customers were ready for their bed. Very strong beers such as barley wines were only rarely sold on draught and generally came in third-pint bottles or 'nips'. The bottle was also the usual export format, although exports weren't and aren't a very significant part of the beer trade.

The price premium bottled beers commanded was an attractive opportunity for the brewers. Some started brewing prestige bottle-only brands to take advantage of it: Newcastle Brown, one of the most famous bottled beers in the world, first went on sale in 1927. Others produced draught and bottled variants of the same brand at different strengths: Adnams Broadside, for example, was launched in 1972 at 4.7 per cent ABV on draught and a luxurious 6.3 per cent in bottle. By these means branded bottled beers acquired a cachet they have never lost; but for a long time their best sale was in the take-home trade, which was until recent times a tiny fraction of the trade in volume and even more so in value.

This is now changing, thanks in large part to the gradual rise over the last 30 years in the availability of and familiarity with an inexhaustible variety of premium-bottled beers from Belgium, Germany and the US. Specialist alehouses have for years routinely had a chiller cabinet or two full of Trappist beers, lambics and other Continental fancies: in some cases where there is no room for the cabinets behind the counter they have simply been positioned on the customers' side… next to an honesty box! That may be going a bit far, but there are big advantages to be had from stocking a good range of bottles. One is that if you suspect your customers are ready for a dalliance with an Oud Bruin, and if they're prepared for the shock when they see how much you'll have to charge to maintain your gross profit, you can start small.

There are now specialist importers and distributors covering the whole country, and if one of them sees you as a potential long-term prospect they will start you off on a small mixed delivery of half-a-dozen or so cases. They will also advise you on a good starter pack – but do ask your customers first if there are any foreign or bottled beers they have particularly enjoyed. That way you'll achieve two things: you'll more or less guarantee a quick turnaround for your first order, and you'll also initiate a dialogue with your customers, asking them to nominate brands they'd like you to stock; perhaps establishing a scoring system; even holding tutored tastings on slack nights. Then there are incremental purchases by customers stocking up before they set off for home, which all add to turnover, but the main thing is the conversation exotic and unusual bottled beers can inspire.

Don't make the mistake, though, of stocking brands that supermarkets already carry: the price differential will be jaw-dropping and you don't want to make comparisons too easy! Minimising overlap with the supermarkets does more than just conceal the price-gap: it also emphasises your superior ability to stock weird and wonderful confections both from overseas and from British craft brewers. And if any particular brands turn out to be duds, you can sell them off at cost without loss: you only had a single case, after all.

Talk of craft brewers brings us to the subject of cans. Once they were taboo in pubs, but not any more. We're not talking here about the mainstream cut-price multipacks depressingly but accurately known to supermarket beer-buyers as 'slabs'; we're talking about (mainly) high-quality beers from craft brewers. Having decided that the liquid was more important than the packaging those cheeky imps in the brewing world started putting their beers in cans – in many cases using the services of a mobile canning company established precisely for the purpose – to much acclaim. If your customers are ready for it, and the younger beer-drinkers have shown that they most definitely are, then sell it to them.

NLA beers

Soft drinks have always been a problem for mostly beer-drinking males, whose principle reasons for abstinence have traditionally been the entirely negative ones that they are either driving or on a diet. The trouble is that beer drinkers are used to malt, and in quantity: sweet and mainly fruit-flavoured soft drinks are like being offered a sherbet lime when what they wanted was a bacon sandwich. All sorts of shifts have been tried both by dieters and 'designated drivers': tomato juice with lots of Lea & Perrins and tonic water with a good splash of Angostura are certainly not sweet, but the standard single serve of 125ml won't satisfy anyone used to a pint; and anyway, who can drink a pint of tonic water, with or without Angostura? Shandy has always been a good fallback, but lemonade is far too sweet for most beer drinkers. Ginger beer is a better alternative to lemonade for a shandy, but using one of the premium brands makes a pint of it ridiculously expensive – a good reason for carrying a budget version as well!

And so, inevitably, we come to the topic of no and low-alcohol beers or NLAs. A few years ago they would have been the subject of a rather sad footnote to the section on soft drinks, but developments from the Continent have earned them a rather more positive place in the beer section. And the reason for this change in fortunes is that a new generation of NLA has found its way out of the driving/dieting cul-de-sac and into the gym.

Drinking NLAs has always been something of a penance. Lawrie McMenemy could tell us that Barbican was "great, man" in the early 80s adverts until he was blue in the face: it wasn't. People drank it because they were driving or dieting and couldn't face another orange juice. Poor quality was the rock on which even the most determined attempts at brand-building eventually foundered, and as one by one both national and regional brands (with the single exception of Harveys of Lewes) fell by the wayside the market was left almost entirely to imported NLA lagers.

There's never been a shortage of demand, but only recently have brewers really faced up to the challenge of quality, and in very broad terms their answer has been to move away from hi-tech solutions and revisit a more natural method. Basically, there have generally been two ways of making NLA beers. You could either fully brew a beer and then remove the alcohol by dialysis, reverse osmosis or distillation, or you halt the fermentation before it was complete. The bulk of the £50-million-a-year UK NLA beer market was and still is composed of de-alcoholised lagers such as Beck's Blue, Kaliber and Bitburger Drive, but the pendulum seems

Full measure and glassware

The legal measures for draught beer and cider are multiples of a third or a half of an imperial pint (20 fl oz), and assuming the beer-pump isn't metered (which few if any are these days), all glasses need a crown stamp or a CE mark and must either be lined, leaving room for a head, or brim measure. Brim measure is generally used for southern-style ales that aren't poured with much of a head; lined oversized glasses are customary for lagers and northern ales traditionally served with a deep head. This isn't required by law, although customers may ask for and expect to receive a top-up if they're served a deep northern-style head in a brim measure. This has been a matter of much unnecessary controversy for many years, but it's best dealt with pragmatically: you do want the customer and his wallet to come back, don't you?

Glassware is especially important: its cleanliness, its condition – even its design – give customers their first impression of what to expect. Serious beer lovers today will also appreciate you if you keep handled mugs as well as straight glasses: handles are making a comeback because they hold the beer at serving temperature for longer than thin glasses, a fact that true beer-lovers are increasingly aware of. They cost more than thin glasses but last far longer, and as they're almost impossible to break they make far less damaging weapons should a fight break out.

Glassware should always be sparkling but should only be washed in dedicated machines and never in kitchen dishwashers that are also used for other utensils that might have fat on them. Empty used glasses down a separate waste pipe before putting them in the machine. Only use odour-free non-soap

> glass-washing liquids. Always use rinse aid and air-dry the glasses upside-down on a draining rack. Clean glasses should be left until cool before use. Wash new glassware in renovating powder before using them for the first time. Use renovator regularly anyway, as it stops greasy film from building up. If water sticks to the side of newly washed glasses, or if faint crescents of lipstick persist, you're not using it often enough! Finally, throw away any chipped or cracked glasses immediately.

to be swinging towards part-brewed beers and, in particular, part-brewed beers made of more flavoursome grains.

Most German brewers already have a wheat beer in their portfolio that they can simply part-brew. Erdinger alcohol-free weizenbier at 0.4% ABV is one: it rates 120 calories a pint compared to 180–200 calories in a standard alcoholic beer. Krombacher's alcohol-free weizenbier is brewed from the same grist as the 5.3% ABV full-strength version and is Germany's leading brand. Wheat-based NLAs have a key advantage over NLA lagers: wheat malt has distinctive flavours and aromas of its own, so the beers are pleasantly tasty – tasty enough, in fact, to have attracted an aspirational fan-base in their native Germany of younger sportspeople and athletes to whom an NLA is a first choice rather than a distress purchase.

British distributors of these brands are doing their best through sports sponsorships and promotions to tap into the same youthful and fitness-aware market that's flourishing in Germany, Scandinavia and the Low Countries. It's certainly worth stocking NLA wheat beers alongside the usual drivers' lagers; but if you do you will have to promote them yourself with PoS, discounted trials and staff suggestion as awareness is, at the time of writing, fairly low.

The latest innovation, though, is all-British and involves a new twist on part-brewing. This generally leaves a sweetish, unappetising and worty flavour. Brewers such as St

Peter's, Big Drop and Nirvana, however, have adopted a multi-step approach to creating alcohol-free beers that involves tweaking the traditional brewing process at every stage – but only slightly. A grist of mixed malted and unmalted grains, usually including wheat and often rye and oats as well, will be mashed at high temperature to inhibit saccharification and produce a full-bodied but low-gravity wort. Unfermentable lactose may be added to the wort to fill out the mouthfeel and body still further. The wort will be boiled with a very characterful hop grist then fermented with a poor-attenuating yeast, infused with citrus or other flavourings and finally dry-hopped. The result is, or should be, a very tasty beer of 0.5% ABV or less.

Cider

Technically, cider is wine made of apples (just as perry is wine made of pears), but commercially it has always been treated as if it were a subset of beer. Historically cider was the working man's long drink in the regions where it was made, served draught by the pint and as still and as dry as nature intended. Today it has been reinvented as a variant of lager – pasteurised, filtered, carbonated, chilled and watered down to a sessionable 4.5% ABV when its natural strength is closer to 6.5–7 per cent. More recently still it has been reinvented yet again as the latest thing in ready-to-drink, laden with fruit (or fruit flavourings) despite the extra duty this incurs, and is hugely popular among younger drinkers.

All in all, then, the major nationally distributed brands have strayed about as far from the orchard as it's possible to get while still calling themselves cider. To most licensees none of that really matters: mass-produced cider in all its manifestations – whether it's good old Strongbow or Magners or mango and raspberry-flavoured Rekorderlig – is enjoyed by millions, especially in summer, and is quite simply a must-stock. All they have to do is order more before the last lot runs out and remember to keep a vast stock of ice for the Magners.

More interesting, although still a minority taste with low enough public awareness ratings to categorise it as exotic, is what enthusiasts call 'real' cider, what the industry calls 'traditional' cider and what the public persists in calling 'scrumpy'. We are back, then, on the familiar ground of loose, uncertain or downright fictional terminology, for the spectrum within which cider brands identify themselves as 'traditional' is very broad indeed. At one end of the scale is completely natural cider fermented from absolutely pure apple juice (cider apple juice in the west, cooker and eater juice in the east) by the action of naturally occurring yeast, with almost the only human intervention being skilful blending, and which to the novice might seem too tannic or even vinegary. Makers of this sort of cider are proliferating not just in the traditional regions of the West Country, the Western Midlands, the south-east and East Anglia but all over England and Wales; and there are even a few to be found in Scotland where temperate Tayside is a traditional fruit-growing district. The 7,000 litre duty-exempt production limit is a great inducement for many smallholders – and indeed anyone who owns a patch of land – to make cider and perry as a sideline; and although their production is necessarily limited many of these part-timers produce drinks of very good quality. Almost wherever you are nowadays you will find one of these duty-exempt makers near you just waiting for your call; there is also almost bound to be at least one larger more commercial but still artisanal maker within 50 miles.

The output of the vast majority of artisan makers is still and very dry, because when you just leave your cider to get on with things it ferments almost completely. However, most of us have got used to drinking our cider with a bit of sparkle and the leading independents, including Westons, Sheppy's and Thatchers, have created very acceptable carbonated mainstream brands that are quite highly processed but still suit the public's idea of 'traditional' and satisfy the trade's demand for an authentic-looking product that is both stable and consistent.

The public generally thinks of its 'scrumpy' as draught, but in recent years smaller independents have become more and more professional in their packaging and presentation, and offer bottled brands that are hardly processed at all but are still more than acceptable to the unschooled palate. One or two of these are essential in any specialist beer bar. If you have any sort of a garden you can do a brisk cider trade in summer, and if you have a food offering with any pretence to sophistication try offering a medium still traditional cider, reasonably but not excessively chilled, by the carafe, highlighting in your publicity material that it has half the alcohol and half the calories of white wine. Natural cider is absolutely dry and therefore an option for diabetics.

It's also worth noting that traditional West Country ciders made of real cider-apple juice are good keepers on draught even when broached. Their high tannin content and relatively high ABVs kill bacteria and are effective anti-oxidants. Bag-in-box is also becoming a preferred packaging format among smaller makers because it's so simple to handle; from the retailer's point of view bag-in-box also makes the product virtually immortal and eliminates wastage pretty much completely.

Guest ales and promotions

The simplest and most common way of promoting your beer is to keep changing it. A changing guest policy, however modest, still has to be promoted, though – people can't be expected to guess. Indoors, the standard 'forthcoming guest ales' blackboard can be made interactive simply by leaving

Case study
The Rake, Southwark, London

Borough Market at the southern end of London Bridge is the undoubted current epicentre of food fashion in Britain. The place is a temple of sensory delight, the capital city of cheeses, seafood, all manner of meats, cakes and pastries, of chocolates and sweets, wines and spirits... and of beer. Utobeer, an offshoot of a Bermondsey-based beer importer of the same name owned by Richard Dinwoodie and Mike Hill, started trading in the market at Christmas 1999 with a mere 50 artisan bottled beers, mainly from Belgium and Germany. Beers of this kind – the term 'craft' hadn't been invented at that time but the underlying values of quality and diversity certainly had – weren't exactly a rarity in 1990s London: legendary beer shops such as the one attached to Pitfield Brewery in Hoxton were fairly liberally sprinkled around the capital. But although connoisseurs and aficionados never need to run short of supplies, knowledge and understanding of the myriad styles of Continental and American beer sold in these specialist shops was hardly mainstream.

Utobeer's place in history was a consequence of its place in Borough Market: food tourists flocked and still flock to it from all over the country, returning home laden with purchases and stories. Utobeer put weird and wonderful beers right at the heart of food fashion and became, unarguably, one of the pillars of today's craft beer market. And then, in 2006, Utobeer had a beautiful bouncing baby. Between the market itself and Southwark Cathedral, unseen by the general public, lies the stall-holders' car park, and on the edge of that is a mid-Victorian pub, originally the Old King's Head and later the Jubilee Café, which was the stallholders' café and WC. By 2006 the café had been empty for some years, so Richard and Mike took it over, transformed its tiny bar (at 9 x 13 feet even smaller than the

Butcher's Arms, which had opened the previous year) with the aid of a floor-sander and a few pots of paint, and opened it as the Rake. Originally it was intended as a showcase for the importer/wholesaler side of the business, with 130 foreign bottled beers in chillers, seven keg taps and three hand-pumps. And although it wasn't the first such bar – Bar Fringe in Manchester, for example, opened in 1998 and was the precursor of the whole Northern Quarter district of style and craft bars – the Borough Market effect made it a cult hit not just in London but with a reputation nationwide.

Canny marketing cemented the Rake's fame: Myleene Klass did a photoshoot there, which went from forgettable to viral (well, viral for 2007) when the partners cunningly rushed out a statement denying that it was her favourite pub. They also denied ever claiming it was London's smallest, even though it was. They encourage visiting brewers to sign their names on the wall. Leading beer writers hung out there. There are beer festivals and tap takeovers as well, and to cap it all, since the partners can't always be there in person they make sure the staff know the range like the back of their hands and can talk hapless civilians through the terror of ordering from a range of 130 completely unknown beers charmingly and knowledgeably. (That included the beer that hit the headlines in summer 2017 for its price of £13.80 a pint. The howls of media outrage were drowned out by the ringing of the cash register as the beer sold out within hours.)

In 2011 Utobeer extended its empire still further with the opening of a craft brewery of its own complete with bar: Tap East, in Stratford, East London. Five years after that the retail estate of market stall and two pubs had grown to the extent where the original business, the importing and wholesaling side, was sold to Yorkshire-based opposite number James Clay.

a space (and a bit of chalk) for customers' suggestions, and can be accompanied by previous guests' pump clips. Outdoors, an A-board coupled with an announcement in the local CAMRA branch newsletter should generate extra traffic. Always encourage customers to try before they buy, and be ready (and make sure your bar staff are ready) to talk them through each beer and its brewery. It may seem like a lot of effort, especially if your guest selection is not all that exciting, but any opportunity to chat up your customers is not to be missed.

The big beer promotion for most pubs is the annual or biannual beer festival, and although many micropubs do hold indoor mini-festivals we're rather assuming that as a converted shop you don't have much outdoor space. If you do, remember that you can't legally make any actual sales outdoors without a TEN or let people take their drinks on to the pavement without a pavement licence from the county council.

An increasingly popular alternative to the beer festival, especially for smaller set-ups like yours, is the brewery take-over when you hand over as many of your pumps/taps/chiller cabinet facings as possible to a single craft brewer. You make a bit of a fuss of it in the CAMRA branch newsletter, send a press release to the local paper and perhaps if you're feeling flush take a paid-for ad in the local community/listings magazine. Give plenty of warning on your chalkboards both indoor and out. Decorate the bar with some of the brewery's PoS (if it doesn't have any there's something wrong with it) and leave plenty of its pamphlets and leaflets lying about. Invite the brewer to give some spiel in the mid-evening when the bar is beginning to get busy and to be on hand to schmooze. This is a form of promotion that costs you nothing at all (unless you take out the aforementioned ad), but generates a lot of interest among the people you're trying to engage. And never forget, of course, that this kind of promotion is a traffic-builder: customers who are interested in beer will bring with them companions who aren't that fussy but who will come back if the general ambience and the rest of the offering suits them.

Then there's the tasting paddle. This, although well suited to the role, is not an archaic instrument of chastisement but the sampling menu of the beer world. And it really is a paddle, too, with a blade big enough to hold several sampling glasses of different beers (known for some reason as a 'flight') for customers to try. Beer paddles have become very popular in American craft beer bars: they're great talking points, and customers can sample a good range without getting drunk or spending all their money. This is partly due to the fact that Americans are used to tiny samples: the glasses at the Great American Beer Festival hold just a single fluid ounce! The drawback in the UK is that the smallest legal measure for draught beer is a whopping third of a pint or 6.6 fl oz, which rather defeats the object. Many bars do actually offer these oversized tasting flights, but to make the idea work as originally intended you would really have to persuade customers to share by drawing the beers into legal measures and supplying shot glasses into which they can legally decant the tasting samples themselves. It's a lot of faff, but if you're serious about your beer the concept is definitely worth a try. And of course, it's another talking point…

Matthew Clark

The link without the chains	113
Britain's best wine cellar	114
Have a beer. No: have 900 beers	115
High spirits	116
Liqueurs, vermouths and bitters	117
Mixers and minerals	118

Sponsored feature

Matthew Clark: the link without the chains

While many sectors of the hospitality industry are facing challenging times – traditional wet led pubs and casual dining outlets probably the most prominent among them – independent specialists are on a roll. Ale driven micropubs, craft beer bars, wine and tapas bars, cocktail lounges and licensed cafés seem to have hit the sweet spot with their quirky niche appeal and their rock bottom running costs. To go it alone successfully their operators – which means you! – have to be canny people with their ears to the ground, and with the kind of direct connection with their consumers that bigger concerns sometimes find difficult to maintain. Get it right and you have a living you love, with no one on your back.

But it would be wrong to assume that single outlet owner operators like you don't need easy access to a supply chain that can whisk top of the range products in all categories from all over the world straight to your door at the click of a mouse. Your purchasing requirements may be much more modest than those of the nearest branch of the giant multiple you're competing against; but because you're small, because you're idiosyncratic, because you've promised your consumers a smorgasbord of unknown artisan brands from over the hill and far away, often on short rotations, you have even more need of a modern, efficient, and above all big supplier with tentacles all around the globe. Independent specialists need exactly the same services and support as lessees and managers!

And that, essentially, is what we are. For independent retailers Matthew Clark is the link to just about everything you'll ever need – but without the chains.

We were founded in 1810 as a wines and spirits broker (or importer and wholesaler, in modern parlance) in Great Tower Street, conveniently close to the London docks, by the son of the Inspector General of Imported Liquors & Distillery at the Port of London. In 1990, after six generations of family ownership, we floated on the stock market, moved to Bristol, and quickly became what we are today – Britain's premier licensed trade wholesaler, with 14 depots serving 15,000 accounts and stocking an astonishing range of 7,000 lines. .

But all that history and all those decades of family ownership don't add up to a company hidebound by tradition: we didn't get to be over 200 years old without becoming expert at surfing the wave of the new. Just look at the product range and see for yourself.

Britain's best wine cellar

As a dedicated wine supplier to the on trade, we have longstanding relationships with hundreds of winemakers around the world, and each year we carefully construct a list of wines produced by small family owned wineries as well as many produced ethically along with top consumer requested brands.

The 1,400 wines we choose for our range are selected solely with our on trade customers in mind; but we don't leave it at that: we aim to support you in every aspect of your wine sales. To make our range as easy to navigate as possible, we've segmenting our wine range using our own classification of different wine styles, Wine Expression. In 2009 we won Wine List of the Year and Wine Educator of the Year at the International Wine Challenge awards and went on to launch our Wines of Distinction premium range in 2011. We introduced our team of Wine Development Specialists in2012 to work with you to develop wine ranges, offer advice on selling more wine and educating your staff. Since then we have trained hundreds of customers and staff through Wine & Spirit Education Trust Foundation, Intermediate and Advanced level every year.

We always aim to offer an unrivalled selection of wines to suit your requirement for both the familiar and the eclectic. More than 500 in the range are exclusive to us, and our list is always changing to reflect shifts in consumer preferences. We continue to pioneer iconic and premium wines from both the new and old worlds, and showcase a collection filled with new wave winemakers as well as established heroes from famous wine regions. We know that individuality and innovation are important to you, so we have strengthened our range of wines sourced from less familiar European regions such as Burgenland, Austria and Hampshire. ...The list is brimming with treasures, over 750 vegan and vegetarian wines and more than 50 organic wines, and we hope you and your customers enjoy discovering them.

Sponsored feature

At Matthew Clark we continue to focus on bringing our wines to life in an engaging way, and our dedicated, experienced team of Wine Development Specialists do just that! Providing training and category insights in maximising range and trade up opportunities, our team supports customers nationwide. We strongly believe that investing in training and education adds real value in supporting your wine offering. Your account manager will be happy to help facilitate the right support for your team.

We can also help with the design and production of your wine list: our excellent in house design studio can produce a bespoke professional list to match your operational requirements. We are confident that we can offer unrivalled choice, quality and value right across your range, and we wish you all the very best in the years ahead.

Have a beer. No: have 900 beers!

Whatever your speciality in the licensed trade, you can't do without beer. Beer is the world's favourite alcoholic drink: the most patrician of gentlemen's clubs and the most vinous of wine bars will have a few cases kicking about somewhere. One day, one of your customers is going to fancy nothing more desperately than a nice cold beer; and even if your speciality is tequila based cocktails and you know very little about beer it will earn you brownie points if you can come up with something really nice.

And that's where the art lies. There are thousands and thousands of beers to choose from. Stocking the obvious selection if you're, say, a licensed café, of one or two well known national lager brands, an ale and a stout is as easy as breathing and indeed, it's what most operators do. But even if beer isn't really your schtick you can make your mark with a more distinctive and idiosyncratic selection. The same is true if beer really is your schtick: however knowledgeable you thought you were, you can still be literally spoilt for choice. You don't want to end up picking names out of a hat. You need triage. And that's where we come in.

Our range of 900 beers of all styles and colours from the palest pilsner to the darkest stout and in all formats and sizes from can to cask has been carefully selected by our own expert buyers so that every beer you order from Matthew Clark is guaranteed to be the best of its kind and in the finest possible condition. Our online beer list is categorised to help you zoom in on what's right for your outlet, and to help you navigate the shifting sands of the craft revolution we have a special Boutique Beers range of more than 130 brands that changes every year and now focuses on the mainly lighter, hoppier IPAs, pilsners, golden ales, saisons and sours favoured by younger drinkers. To make sure we're right on trend we've called on the advice and guidance of top beer writers such as Melissa Cole and Pete Brown. We also offer marketing activities tailored to drive sales in your outlet and regular opportunities under the Boutique Beers banner to meet the artisan brewers themselves.

Our cider range also reflects what's hot in the market, with 200 brands embracing every style from traditional draught to up to the minute flavoured varieties including firm favourites like Magners, new wave draught fruit cider taking the market by storm with brands like Magners dark fruit, and modern ciders appealing to new cider drinkers with quirky humour-led brands such as Orchard Pig.

High spirits

When the first Matthew Clark set up his wines and spirits brokerage in 1810, one of the first import brands he signed was Martell, a Cognac that hadn't been (legally) available in Britain since the outbreak of war with France in 1793. Matthew showed how on the ball he was by crossing the Channel only weeks after the Emperor Napoleon was deposed and packed off to Elba in April 1814 – and his successors are just as on it as the founder was.

The big buzz in the spirits world today is of course gin. Staid and unfashionable with little going on in the way of innovation, gin took off as a fashionable and even exciting spirit after the launch of Hendricks, with its botanicals of cucumber and rose, by whisky giant William Grant of

Glenfiddich fame back in 1999. And how things have changed since then! Not only have big distillers launched new gins with all sorts of weird and wonderful botanicals, – rhubarb, violet and orange being current favourites – but new microdistilleries with equally eclectic tastes have sprung up in every corner of the country too. For the first time in centuries there are now more distilleries in England than Scotland –166 to 160 at time of writing – and gin exports have soared from £288m in 2010 to £612m in 2018. Whatever kind of operation you run you need to reflect the vogue, and here at Matthew Clark we carry more than 850 domestic and imported gins from Adnams to Zymurgorium, all fully described and all commanding a very handsome GP.

But it's not all about gin. We have another 3,000 spirit brands of all varieties and nationalities in our portfolio, allowing you not just to compete strongly in today's market but to anticipate tomorrow's. At time of writing rum is following hot on gin's tail in terms of trade innovation and consumer excitement: we currently stock more than 350 – not just dark, gold, white and spiced, but pisco and cachaça too. Our 150 strong range of premium whiskies includes single malts from Ireland and Japan and, critically, a highly competitive showing of top shelf American bourbons and ryes too.

Liqueurs, vermouths and bitters

So often when trying to establish and maintain a credible cocktail offering it's the fiddly bits that let you down. You've got your moody lighting, your intimate booths, your metre square dance floor; you've got a brace of accomplished mixologists – the DJs of drink – shaking everything they've got in their chrome and ebony batcave; but what you don't got is a single bottle of Taylors Velvet Falernum, because your regular supplier doesn't stock it. So, no Swizzles for your regular ravers tonight.

Here at Matthew Clark, though, we understand that any cocktail operation, however modest or specialised, depends on a reliable supply of a huge array of liqueurs, syrups, purées, vermouths, bitters and other potions that you used to see gathering dust in sticky half empty bottles in dark and cobwebby corners of the barback. Now they're front and centre again. That's why we cover the waterfront with nearly 300 of them from Advocaat to Zuidam, taking in some of the world's most prestigious fruit liqueur ranges in their entirety, such as Marie Brizard, Angostura orange bitters, more vermouths than you knew existed and, yes, Velvet Falernum.

Everything to keep your mixologists happy, in fact; and you know how temperamental they can be. And our screw tops actually undo!

Mixers and minerals

No matter what kind of bar you run, your favourite customer is going to be the regular G&T drinker. Nothing in your range commands a better GP than spirits – a bottle of topshelf gin or single malt whisky that cost £30 wholesale can return £5 a shot or £150 a bottle – except soft drinks. In fact the soft drinks that used to be an afterthought (remember when they were called 'pop'?!) many years ago are now such a core item that if everybody in the world went sober in October and dry in January you could probably shut up shop for the other 10 months.

Ginmania has certainly worked wonders for the soft drinks industry, creating a huge demand for premium mixers both in traditional guises – principally tonic and bitter lemon – and also in an unending variety of new flavours. But the tide of innovation in soft drinks long predates the arrival of the first artisan gin, Sipsmith's, in 2007. Belvoir Fruit Farms elderflower pressé arrived in 1984; Fentiman's, a ginger beer which had gone out of production in the mid 1960s, was revived by the original family in 1989; at the same time a Cotswold based home winemaker, Kit Morris, turned his hobby into a business and launched Bottle Green elderflower cordial. Fever Tree, perhaps the leading name in premium soft drinks and mixers, was launched in 2005 by the former boss of Plymouth Gin, Charles Rolls.

These and the countless new wave brands that have hit the market are a world away from the sugar stiff orangeade of yore in that they're principally intended for adults: adults who agree with Charles Rolls that a

Sponsored feature

premium spirit deserves a premium mixer; adults who are driving; adults who are careful of their health and weight; and also adults who just enjoy the flavours. Not that there aren't plenty of equally innovative soft drinks for kids.– but adults are the key market in that they are more demanding of variety and generally have a higher spend.

To help your business stay ahead of the curve we now carry an astonishing 700 soft drinks – yes, even we were a bit surprised when we counted – of just about every description you can imagine and some you possibly can't, and in every conceivable format. For everybody who ever comes into your bar and for some reason doesn't want a double helles prune IPA or a belladonna forward artisan gin tonight.

At Matthew Clark, we go beyond delivering drinks. We realise that our work shouldn't stop there. For us, serving that perfect drink is part of a journey that starts with our buyers sourcing the best products the world has to offer and only ends when a satisfied customer has finished the glass. That's why at every step of the way we make sure the experience matters. Using our 200 years of history, sourcing and supplying every type of drink, we support our customers with what they need to turn products into profits. That means offering accredited training, marketing support, and business tools, as well as the reliable service and enviable range any bar owner would expect.

All of our customers benefit from a dedicated account team, comprising of an account manager that is always close at hand and marketing managers and product specialists that help our customers when they need it. Underpinning all we do is our unequalled delivery network that gives us the ability to make outlet deliveries on a next day basis from our own depot network. Delivering customers the perfect glass or bottle every time is as important to us as it is to you, so you can be assured that each depot is filled with thousands of products, from the classic to the quirky and everything in between. To find out more, arrange a chat with one of our team by visiting

www.matthewclark.co.uk/newaccount

05

Up spirits

Financial planning	123
Gross profit	124
The mixologist	132
Staff training and retention	136
The bar-back	138

Case Studies

Dare Café/A Bar Below, Leeds	*130*
The Wharf, Potterspury	*134*

Ale-oriented micropubs probably come to mind first when we think of bars that have been carved out of old shops. That's because they tend to pop up in unexpected but highly visible places, and often in equally unexpected but highly visible buildings. One, for instance, was a Christian reading room, another was a cricket pavilion, while a third was a fisherman's workshop right on the quayside. Former railway arches, ticket offices, waiting rooms and public toilets are particularly favoured as atmospheric conversion sites.

It might come as a surprise to learn, then, that cocktail bars are actually more numerous than micropubs, although in many cases oddly less conspicuous. Some hide in plain sight amid all the city-centre restaurants and nightclubs in the neon quarters where outlets come and go. These are the Friday and Saturday night party bars, selling pitchers of Woo Woo to undiscriminating revellers who dream of Ibiza but will settle for Wetherspoons. Others, the 'speakeasies' of modern parlance, take delight in finding the obscurest nooks and crannies of the modern metropolis: on the top floor of a skyscraper, down an alley next to the Salvation Army parachurch, on the mezzanine of the former Corn Exchange. Sometimes they will open only to those who know the secret password (which would be more of a secret if it weren't published on their website and all the local review sites).

Like craft brewers and fusion chefs, their mixologists compete to come up with the most unlikely concoctions blending the weirdest and wackiest ingredients they can source or make. Many of the best-known live in fruitful symbiosis in parts of hotels – cellar bars, snooker rooms, roof terraces – that were underused but whose true potential the hotel managers themselves felt unable to unlock. What all these variations of the genre have in common is that they cost far, far more to establish than a humble micropub.

Financial planning

In licensing and planning terms, all shop conversions are equal. But once you have your change of use permission and premises licence, the similarities end. We all know about the artisan-distilling boom, how gin became hip and how whole ranges of premium mixers have been developed to complement it. But if the mere mechanics of setting up a spirits-based bar are the same as any other – rent a shop, tart it up, get a licence and change of use permission, open the doors – it's going to be a far greater capital investment than a micropub because such bars usually require high-end conceptualisation, design and finish, repurposed cable bobbins and freight pallets being comparative rarities in the world of cocktails. Then there's a frightening array of sundries such as expensive glassware, cocktail shakers, swizzle sticks and more accessories and gadgets than you can imagine. Finally, of course, before you can open you need to pay for a very broad range of extremely pricey stock (this is where the company credit card comes in handy!).

Meanwhile your overheads are going to be much higher than a micropub's, partly because you're going to need expert staff and plenty of them. And of course if your venue is strategically located in a suitably bustling part of the city centre, both its rent and consequently its business rates are going to be high – possibly sky-high. Matching the cost of a site to its potential is a balancing act that has defeated many operators. You will also find that cocktail customers demand a wider range of services than micropub customers: if you want to keep the duration of visit and spend per head up to a reasonable level you'll need to shell out a lot on music in a highly-competitive environment. You might even find, perhaps to your dismay, that the music your DJs play is a stronger identifier and a more powerful attraction than your cocktails. And DJs who know what they're about don't come cheap.

Perhaps for these reasons many urban cocktail bars are actually branches of small multiples with trading experience in the locality, a good track record and existing cash flow to reassure investors and lenders. For an inexperienced newcomer to open such a high-risk operation is inviting trouble; on the other hand spirits-based operations outside established entertainment zones are unusual because although entry may be much cheaper, there's no guarantee that the custom is there. Perhaps that's why most of these type of operations occupy underused spaces in existing pubs and hotels, where they are usually set up by the publican or hotelier but might just as well be sub-let to an enterprising third party.

Gross profit

The generic publican's best friend in the whole world is the habitual gin and tonic drinker, because the products with the biggest margins in the trade are spirits and soft drinks. But while spirits and soft drinks sales may be the publican's icing on the cake, they're the bar owner's bread and butter. We'll talk about soft drinks later, but even a bottle of well-aged single malt or craft-distilled gin at £30 wholesale retailing at modest £4 a measure will return £120; in the right location and with the right clientele it can and should fetch significantly more. Many cocktail bars start charging at £9 and go well into double figures, but when you consider the number of ingredients and the amount of work that go into them, prices like this are far from exorbitant.

But luxury spirits, it seems, are pretty much recession-proof anyway. In bad times it's the poor – not just consumers with little spare cash but also the pubs and brands that rely on them – that go to the wall while the well-off not only continue to spend as before but remain just as willing to trade up: in fact, on-trade premium spirits sales grew by 19 per cent in the year October 2015–October 2016, and in the preceding decade their value share of on-trade liquor sales rose from 16 per cent to 24 per cent – a growth significantly boosted by the fact that duty on spirits had been frozen in 10 of the preceding 20 budgets, with a consequent collapse in the traditionally high price differential between beer and spirits. Everybody will be aware of the craft-distilling boom that has been helped along by this succession of freezes (and also by the replacement in 1993 of the archaic system of charging duty on the gravity of unfermented wash with charging it at the factory gate). More than 150 small distilleries have opened in Britain so far this century, making mostly gin but also whisky, apple brandy, grape brandy, spiced rum, grappa, pálinka and even a vodka distilled from fermented whey. But what's significant is that nearly all of the newcomers post-date the credit crunch; not a single one of them at the time of writing has gone bust; and they major on super-premium products at £30+ a bottle. So confident is the spirits industry that Scotland is bursting with new whisky distilleries even though it takes a minimum of three years (and in practice much longer) to make any sort of return at all. Clearly, then, consumers like what the craft distillers are doing, and in the right kind of outlet an adventurous range presented properly is a very potent attraction.

Not only is the mark-up per bottle big, the risk is small. You can buy artisanal spirits by the bottle from a host of online retailers, which makes trialling new product lines an economic proposition; and although the price will be rather higher than you'd pay wholesale there's still an excellent profit to be had, and sluggish sales of an unpopular experiment will be offset by its keeping qualities. True, opened bottles of spirits do deteriorate in time. Depending on the alcohol content – and most premium spirits are bottled at more than the standard 40% ABV – and the surface area and depth of liquid in the bottle, it will eventually 'collapse': the ethanol will evaporate and collect in the headspace to dissipate when the bottle is opened; and at the same time the flavour components will begin to oxidise, leaving a weak, mushy liquid good for nothing but soil-conditioning. But the process can take up to two years, and you can surely sell 30 measures in two years even of the most egregious of mistakes. If in doubt – for example, if a bottle seems to have been hanging around for a suspiciously long time – don't serve it without taking the tiniest sip yourself first.

Outlay and overheads

Running a fully-fledged cocktail bar is a highly specialised business. Even hotel bars that call themselves cocktail bars tend to stop short of the full implications of the name (except the cocktail bars in very swish hotels, that is). For the skills required by competent mixologists make them more like chefs than humble bar staff, and the range of ingredients and equipment demanded to produce anything but the most basic concoctions make the cocktail bar more like a kitchen than a lounge.

How much you spend on decorating and equipping your bar is, of course, up to you: the sky's the limit. But in terms of capital commitment there's one item of expenditure that will brook no corner-cutting or cheese-paring, and that's your ingredients. When opening a micropub you can get away with laying in two or three firkins of each of your six chosen cask ales at £80-odd or £1,440 in total, and investing about half that amount in cider, wine and soft drinks. A smidgeon over £2,000, then, should be enough for your first week's trading and if you've done your sums right it ought to bring in a gross profit of 60 per cent or £5,000.

The cocktail bar's first week's worth of stock, however, will cost rather more than that, not because you need much more of it to keep the highball glasses full but because you need to stock so many different lines, and as a new customer you can't expect any discounts. That equates to 20 whiskies (minimum), 20 gins, 20 vodkas, white rums, dark rums, brandies (various), vermouths, 50–60 liqueurs, bitters (and not just Angostura, either!), cordials, fruit juices, grenadine, Champagne... Of course, the variety you buy in depends entirely on the menu you've planned: you don't have to be as insanely innovative and experimental as, say The Gibson bar in Clerkenwell, central London, whose cocktails include such abstruse ingredients as fermented potato ketchup, fennel wine, cauliflower and clay cordial (no, really), orris and nougat cream and fudge sherry cordial. But still, this is a massive array by any standards and to start with at least, you need more than you're going to need.

And as for the accessories! Not just hardware such as shakers and swizzle sticks and jiggers and a bewildering array of glassware – by which, if you are to have any credibility at all, you must not be bewildered – but also consumables: purpose-printed mats, cocktail sticks and umbrellas, maraschino cherries, olives, silverskins, fresh mint leaves, fresh fruit... pick up any book of cocktail recipes and the ingredients listed on the first 10 pages alone will be enough to make your accountant's hair stand on end.

You could easily be looking at spending £12,000–15,000 on stock and consumables to keep you trading through your first week; and although a great amount of that will carry over into subsequent weeks, that level of investment makes even the 70–80 per cent GP obtainable on a bottle of spirits look like rather a shaky foundation (a little ray of sunshine here is that when mixing a cocktail of three liquids or more excepting water, you don't have to stick to legal measures, which stretches your margin a little further). What all this boils down to is that unlike the micropub operator, you will almost certainly have to trade at a loss for the first few weeks. A good fat float is therefore vital, and judicious use of a company credit card if you can get one is also more than

Ice

What is it about British pubs and ice? It's not expensive, yet the traditional publican doles it out as if it were rationed in round-edged half-melted shapeless little blobs from a plastic tub that's grudgingly refilled only when the last few solid specks are floating on a slick of cold water. But ice is not an afterthought. Ice is not a luxury. Ice is a staple that should be lavished generously on customers without stint or question unless, that is, they're drinking rare Cognac or a well-aged single malt, in which case a question is recommended!

It's not only the quantity of ice you will need that matters: quality counts too. If you want clear, clean and hard ice, don't make it from tap water unless it's been filtered or boiled first, especially in hard water areas. Simply boiling it will settle out any limescale, and a common or garden office water cooler will filter 15–20 litres of tap water at a time (and if for any special reason you wanted to use spring water to make your ice – if Madonna was in the neighbourhood, say – a 15 litre returnable carboy can cost as little as £8).

As you will doubtless know, ice comes in all shapes and sizes, each with its appropriate application. The basic 2.5cm/1in cube works better in the shaker than more fanciful forms because it has the optimum surface area. It is also, because of its size, preferred in shallow glasses especially the classic cocktail glass. The bigger rock, with sides of 7.5cm/2.5in, looks splendid in larger tumblers – an Old-Fashioned glass, say. Rocks melt very slowly because of their mass; they also cool spirit-heavy and liqueur-rich cocktails, which contain little or nothing from the chiller cabinet, quickly and thoroughly. Even longer lasting is the ice ball, because of its relatively small surface area. For highly specialised mixtures such as cold punch you can chill an entire bowl with an ice block made in a Tupperware container. At the other end of the spectrum, cracked, crushed or shaved ice can be made in a blender or (much more satisfyingly) smashed up between two clean cloths using a steak mallet or rolling pin. A tip here is to make the ice with carbonated water: the CO_2 bubbles will create myriad little holes in the ice, which weaken it and make the smashing process a lot easier. You can smash it as coarsely or as finely as you like: coarse for a traditional Julep, very fine for an alcoholic snow cone.

You can give your ice an extra flourish by infusing the water with a flavoured cordial before freezing, or dying it or adding a flower to each mould. But do be careful about hygiene. Ice does not kill bacteria, and many's the time Environmental Health Officers have tested ice samples only to find them suffused with the most lethal varieties. Meticulous hand-hygiene is essential; boiled water will be sterile; and icemakers, moulds, scoops and buckets must all be thoroughly washed in anti-bacterial cleaner after every single trading session.

Case study
Dare Café/A Bar Below, Leeds

No matter how eclectic, idiosyncratic, individualistic and quirky they may appear, most of the cocktail bars that now seem to outnumber old-fashioned pubs in our city centres aren't independent units with identities created by eclectic, idiosyncratic, individualistic and quirky entrepreneurs. They almost always turn out to be branches of small but well-funded multiples, and even though the parent companies are usually independently owned and locally based, the bar's design, personality and atmosphere don't flow from the freewheeling, iconoclastic and ironical imagination of a maverick owner-operator. They're very carefully and skilfully designed by highly professional practitioners and are intended to be different enough to stand out... but not too far out.

This is not intended as a criticism, more as a reflection on the capital investment required and the overheads to be met in order to enter the cocktail bar arena and trade profitably in it. Compared to a micropub or even a wine bar, it's a completely different order of financial magnitude. City-centre rents are high, and consequently there's no chance of exemption from business rates. The premises have to be big enough to accommodate a dance floor of sorts, equipped with DJ station and very expensive lights and sound system and to have enough space behind the bar for a crew of mixologists to shake their shakers. And as already mentioned both DJs and mixologists have to be paid, too. Small wonder, then, that independent entrepreneurs aren't queuing up to open their own cocktail bars. However committed you are to the proposition that artisan spirits command both a market and margins that make them a very attractive business proposition, it's much easier and cheaper to put it into practice if you already own a bar.

Dare Café has been treating the largely student and metropolitan population of Headingley in Leeds to hardcore Mexican (and Italian, for those less tolerant of chillies) cuisine since 1994, and the 52-cover has not only established but also maintained its five-star review rating ever since. It was only in 2010 that the decision was made to convert the small basement into a bar with room for about 40 customers at a squeeze; but with access only possible through the restaurant it never managed to establish its own separate identity and was mainly used for private parties.

Then in 2016 proprietor Ali Storr decided on a substantial upgrade and a high-visibility relaunch that would reinvent A Bar Below, as she christened it, as a cosy but upmarket hangout for the area's younger crowd. The refit was made less complicated and more affordable by the fact that Dare Ltd already owned the premises and that all the necessary licensing and planning permissions were in place; but as Headingley is already well-supplied with student bars of one kind or another, Ali planned to differentiate A Bar Below by injecting a note of sophistication. That meant no skimping on the design and decor, which together created a cooler, more mellow ambience than most of its local rivals; it also meant introducing cocktails and stocking a good selection of artisan gins, starting with the Masons range from neighbouring Harrogate.

Not everything, of course, went entirely to plan. "We stopped making cocktails quite early on because although everybody loved them they were too difficult and time-consuming because we simply didn't have space for more than one mixologist," says Ali. "The gins were slow to take off, but we kept working at it with gin tastings and gin nights and we've been gradually increasing our range." Regular open mic nights also proved a

> popular attraction, which necessitated stocking a wider range of beers, and in its first year A Bar Below increased its opening nights from three a week to four. "It was slow-going getting the word out that we'd turned our old cellar bar into a venue in its own right," admits Ali. "An awful lot of people didn't even know we had a cellar bar!" But word of mouth and repeat custom gradually built up the numbers, as they do when you've got the offering right, and at the time of writing Ali is working on reintroducing a cocktail menu, which will probably be modest to start with but might well develop. And in the meantime she has discovered a positive side effect she hadn't expected. "Customers still have to come through the restaurant to get to the bar, so a lot of new people have had a chance to check out the café as they're going to the bar," she says. "That means that the bar hasn't only generated extra revenue – it's also increased footfall in the restaurant!"

merely helpful. But this is very much a long-haul business, so set your sales targets realistically, strive to stick to them and keep your nerve.

The mixologist

Another difference between the micropub and the cocktail bar is staff. Most micropubs don't need any. All cocktail bars do. And mixologists aren't living-wage casuals, either: at time of writing experienced applicants were being offered 35–50 per cent above the national living wage, with good packages of benefits to boot. Of course your wage bill will be to an extent subsidised by tips; even so the cocktail bar owner (and restaurateur, for that matter) operates on a completely different plane from the micropublican when it comes to employing and paying staff. It's therefore very important not to make assumptions about staffing but to do your sums very carefully.

So, for your £10–£12 per hour, what kind of output can you expect from an experienced mixologist? According to American restaurant and catering consultant Jerry Prendergast, writing in *Forbes* magazine in 2012: "The other night I sat at a bar and watched an experienced Mixologist take four minutes to make a specialty cocktail, not including the time spent taking the order, ringing it up, collecting money or running a credit card. To be fair, let's say specialty drinks generally take three minutes to make. Applying this to some average pricing (high for some places and low for others), and assuming 50 per cent of a mixologist's time is spent actually making drinks, how much revenue is earned per hour in each category?

- Wine by the glass – $8. Average 60 pours per hour = $480.
- Draft beer – $6. Average 40 pours per hour = $240.
- Classic Martini – $9. Average 30 pours per hour = $270.
- Special cocktails – $12. Average 10 pours per hour = $120.

Given these higher costs, is the hype, the show and the overall hipness of these drinks worth it?"

To be fair to the mixologist, a return of $120 (at 2012 prices – say $150 or £110 at the time of writing) on his or her £12/hour salary isn't bad providing your other costs are under control. In many cocktail bars, mixologists generate considerable additional revenue by running master classes on slack evenings at anything from £25–£40 per head. (As well as highlighting the costs involved, Jerry Prendergast's expert calculations will also help you with your business plan by working out how many mixologists you're likely to need).

Case study
The Wharf, Potterspury

The great advantage to any craft brewer, traditional cidermaker, winemaker or artisan distiller in adding a bar to your brewery/cidery/winery/distillery is that customers don't just come and go but settle down and stay awhile. And if, like so many small-scale food and drink producers, telling is part of selling, then a bar is for you.

Laurence had always set a lot of store on community involvement. In 2009 he started cidermaking in an old canal-side timberyard in Wolverton, Milton Keynes, under the name Virtual Orchard because he had no orchards of his own. Instead he got permission to forage for apples in the town's many public open spaces and also encouraged people with gardens to bag up any surplus apples and bring them along in exchange for juice or cider. Similarly, when he installed his little Portuguese copper pot-still in 2014 he didn't stop at producing 'Aepel drenc' (he uses the Old English to get round EU rules that insist that apple brandy doesn't exist) from his own cider: he started distilling malt wash made by local breweries (new-make available now, matured whisky coming soon) and wine from a local vineyard as well (this latter is currently fast asleep in old Madeira casks and isn't due to be woken up for, oh, ages). Marc is next, apparently – another venture requiring co-operation and collaboration.

Eventually the developers came for the timberyard, and Virtual Orchard/Wharf Distillery had to find a new home – which it did when the biggest unit in a mid-Victorian farmyard converted into shops and studios became available. Assarts Farm at Potterspury in Northamptonshire is part of a 4,000-acre estate that, like so many others, has brand-new barns and sheds. After a minor tussle with Customs, who weren't used to the idea that a still might be sited in a shop and bar, Laurence moved kit and caboodle and promptly got the whole site licensed, enabling him to run outdoor events as well as a licensed gift shop and, of course, a bar with seating for 34 and standing room for another 20-odd. Even the large patch of rough ground that will one day be a perry pear orchard (the '-pury' element in several local place names indicates that pears were once grown here) is licensed. And both shop and bar sell everything: not just Laurence's own cider and spirits but beers, wine, liqueurs, cordials and all kinds of farm, bakery and deli produce from within a 15-mile radius.

For a distillery such as Wharf, the great advantage of possessing a bar is that the margin on on-sales of spirits is so high. True, the overheads are high as well, but the on-sales add enough to the shop revenue to absorb the extra overhead and leave sufficient profit for investment in improving the facility and extending the company's range of operations. As Laurence says, "Of course it helps our bottom line that we can get a better margin in the taproom than we can wholesale or in the shop; that almost goes without saying, but the main point is to encourage people to come to the site to see for themselves what we do and to hear our story. And with the facilities we've got, the space we've got, and the licence we've got the possibilities here are almost endless. Food fairs, music festivals, pop-up restaurants, the travelling pizza oven, cidermaking courses – we can do so much! We're even planning to put up some yurts in the orchard for weddings, too."

The philosopher's stone of any bar, though, is reliable repeat business. Assarts Farm is 366m (1,200ft) from the edge of the village, which already has two pubs. But it's easily walkable, and villagers are beginning to venture out in increasing numbers just for a pint and a pie... rounded off, of course, with a nip or two of Aepel Drenc.

There is one sure way of doubling the technician's productivity, and that's to keep the customers well away from the bar and run table service instead. Waiters will work for the national living wage (£7.83 from April 2018) plus tips; and as one waiter can service several tables, you can easily double each mixologist's output for far less than twice the hourly outlay. Table staff are also better-placed, particularly at peak times, to chat up the customers and keeping the atmosphere going than the white-coated lab technicians behind the bar whose primary focus is on the job in hand rather than the customer.

Staff training and retention

Staff retention is one of the bugbears of the hospitality trade and can add hugely to a bar or hotel's overheads. It's mainly a problem of attitude and tradition: waiters and bar-staff have been seen as part-timers and/or casuals for so long that that's how they see themselves, and their almost random comings and goings generate recruitment costs and cause efficiency problems as the existing staff have to cover vacancies and train newcomers. Investing in your staff and showing that you have high expectations of them is one way of raising their awareness of their professional status and thus earning their loyalty.

All your front-of-house staff should have a strong basic grasp of the tools of their trade. They should all know the difference between Cognac and Armagnac, for instance, and that Calvados doesn't rhyme with Barbados; and if Bunnahabhain is on your list of malts, everyone had better know (a) what it is (b) where it's from and (c) how to pronounce it. You will doubtless be holding weekly meetings with your mixology team – provided you can prize them away from prepping tonight's perfect miniature macédoine of papaya and rambutan, that is – to discuss forthcoming cocktail

> **Mixers**
>
> If you stock super-premium craft-distilled spirits, it makes sense to complement them with premium mixers. There's nothing wrong with the standard Britvic and Schweppes ranges of tonic, soda, ginger ale and juices; indeed it's perhaps doubtful that many customers, given a blind tasting of whisky and sodas using standard sodas and premium competitors such as Fever Tree, Frobisher, Franklin & Sons, Fentimans (strange how many fizzy drinks brands begin with an 'f' – the power of suggestion at work, perhaps?) and Merchant's Heart, could even tell the difference. Some undoubtedly could, but that's not really the point. Successful marketing is a matter of creating and then matching consumer expectations: if your customers see top-shelf spirits they expect top-shelf mixers to match, and it's up to you to see that they get what they expect. And from a purely practical point of view, the new-wave mixers are highly innovative and come in a range of flavours that will make your mixologist yelp with glee.

menus. Encourage as many of the table staff as possible to attend. There should, of course, be a separate daily briefing for table staff as well, but the more in-depth knowledge they possess the more effective they will be. It will also show you who's keen, and who might be worth bringing on and promoting from waiting to mixing.

Many mixologists are freelancers and have paid for their own training. But if you want to enhance your staff retention by holding out the prospect of career development, then paying for the likeliest candidates to attend a Wine and Spirit Education Trust Level 1 Award in spirits is a very good proof of your convictions. It will cost you £150–£200 depending on the provider and whether it's day release or online. The course content is enough to make the candidate a much more useful member of staff and to whet his or her appetite for more.

A WSET Level 3 Award in spirits takes three days and costs rather more – around the £400 mark – and private providers abound, offering their own curricula as well as WSET qualifications. Prices can be high – a three-week European Bartender School course, including 110 instructor-led hours and accommodation, costs £1,800, whereas the Mixology Group breaks its offering down into two-day courses such as Molecular Mixology and Advanced Bartending at around £350 each. You might even consider taking some of these courses yourself, especially in areas where you feel weak.

The bar-back

The space behind the bar is both your shop window and your workplace, and like many workplaces it's inclined to get cluttered. People move around in it. Things get picked up and put down. Liquids get poured. Taps drip. Surfaces get wiped. It's a living, moving space; but here's the rub: it's also located plumb between the public and the most important piece of design in the building, your peacock's fan, your glittering shop window – the bar-back. Even though in a table-service bar customers don't actually make their selection from the bar-back display as they would in a pub, the bar-back must never be anything less than pristine, nor must the ordinary detritus of work be allowed to detract from it, because it's not just a collection of shelves where you lay out your stock so the customers can see what you've got: it must make them want to buy. It must make them drool.

Display is not the only criterion in designing the bar-back and the working space in front of it. You need more room than in a pub, for a start: if two people can scarcely squeeze past each other, your mixologists can't function effectively.

Each can have their own fully-equipped workstation on the counter where all the chopping and splashing and shaking goes on, but given the variety of stock you're likely to carry the widest bar in the world wouldn't allow each workstation to have its own facings of every line. The crew are going to have to pass each other almost constantly as they fetch what they need from the racking behind them and replace it after they finish. They need space (and non-slip flooring).

Glassware, by the way, should never be on show. Everything on the bar-back must delight the eye, so stow the glassware under the counter and on the gantry, where they belong.

06

Wine

Wine's market share 142
Wine and food 144
Wine training 146
Wine service 148
Glassware for wines 150
Wine on tap 154

Case Study
1855 Wine Bar, Oxford *152*

A question: is there still such a thing as a straightforward wine bar? London used to be packed with them once upon a time, especially the City and its western fringes: they were where bankers, lawyers and journalists habitually took their light lunch, along with enough wine to make a tedious afternoon tolerable. A return visit at 5 o' clock helped the train journey home pass in the same pleasantly mild fog.

These really were wine bars, often owned and run by one or other of the independent wine-shippers – Balls Brothers, Corney & Barrow, EJ Rose and others – in which London WC and EC then abounded. You might get a bottled beer there, but rarely would a gentleman ask for one. You couldn't get much in the way of food either: a sandwich or a slightly more elaborate canapé; bangers and mash and one or two other items of nursery food at most. These were the sort of places where, a century ago, you might have found GK Chesterton doing his celebrated Socrates impression, frozen in deepest contemplation having been most unfortuitously struck (after a bottle of claret and half a bottle of port) by a compelling thought. But as I said, that was a century ago. All the wine bars are really restaurants now, even El Vino itself.

Wine's market share

It's ironic that the wine bar and its northern cousin the wine lodge have pretty much disappeared in their purest sense, because wine has never had a greater share of national on-trade liquor sales – and it's a share that's growing. In 2014 wine was worth £5.5 billion to pubs and made up 40 per cent of the value of drinks sold across the on-trade as a whole. The Wine and Spirit Trade Association predicts that wine will increase its value share in pubs from 18 per cent in 2014 to 20 per cent by 2018, while beer's share will shrink from 50 per cent to 47 per cent. Newly-opened bars and pubs, it says, rely more on wine at 22 per cent of wet sales compared to 40.2 per cent for beer than do the more male-oriented old-school generic pubs – the very pubs that are most at risk of closure – with wine sales of just 12.3 per cent compared to 58.5 per cent for beer. *Harpers Wine & Spirit Gazette* has a similar figure: wine's average share of wet sales in the on-licensed premises that had closed in the two years to April 2016 had been 15 per cent, while in the on-licences that opened in the same period it was 22 per cent.

These changes reflect the increasing presence of women, who are greater wine drinkers than their menfolk, and the concurrent growth of food service. Women have always been more significant pub customers than many would allow, but until really quite recently almost always in company with their partners. Today women still use pubs with their partners as they did in the past, and are still almost as unlikely to be casual single pub-goers as they traditionally were; but they are far more likely to go out as part of larger family groups, on women's nights out and hen parties, and in more sophisticated social or professional groups disparagingly known as 'ladies who lunch'.

Dining out has also been a growth sector for some years, despite austerity, and the old-school pub trade as a whole has maintained a strong position in it. Catering market analysts categorise pub dining as 'casual' because the average spend is typically less than £15 a head, and as far as bar snacks and sandwiches are concerned they're right. But pubs also offer what the law designates 'substantial meals' when the preferred beverage is more often wine than beer. This may not be of much relevance to the micropub or cocktail bar operator, but to a bar owner with a fancy for wine it's of more than passing interest, as we shall see.

The wine bars of legal and literary legend disappeared because they were male-dominated and mainly upper-middle class. They were exclusive, like gentlemen's clubs and certain golf and cricket clubs; as recently as 1982 women still weren't allowed to go to the bar and order their own drinks at El Vino on London's Fleet Street. The clientele of these places only felt comfortable with their own kind. But striving to keep potential customers at bay is rarely a formula for commercial success: one by one the Rumpole's retreats of Fleet Street and Farringdon had to choose between closing their doors and upgrading their kitchens. But given current trends it's no surprise that they, or something rather like them, are making a bit of a comeback.

Wine and food

One of the problems with the more common-or-garden wine is that it's hard to get a decent GP on it because everybody knows how much it or an equivalent costs in a supermarket. The only firm piece of wine lore in this book, therefore, is an emphatic 'don't' – that is, don't serve branded wines. There is nothing wrong with Blossom Hill or Hardys or any of the rest of the many branded ranges commonly sold in supermarkets... except that they're sold in supermarkets. Customers know how much they cost, and even if they understand why you have to put on such a big mark-up they still resent it.

The bar-owner's challenge, then, is to create a wine list offering genuine choice while at the same time making a GP of a minimum of 70 per cent and hopefully much more. And since many consumers subconsciously believe that there are two kinds of wine, ordinary home or pub wine and fancy restaurant wine, 70 per cent should be easily achievable. Presented with an unfamiliar label, especially if it's French, they are happy to imagine that a bottle at £21 must be twice as good as one at £10, even though £8 + VAT, or £9.60, was in fact its wholesale price.

If you're running a shoestring operation with minimal overheads, a GP of 70 per cent is adequate provided you're selling enough, but if you're focusing too narrowly on wine, you're unlikely to. Many pure wine bars are actually extensions of upmarket wine merchants where the real payoff comes from private and trade case-sales, but a distinctive food operation is more usually the attention-grabber. That's why tapas bars in many cases don't call themselves wine bars: the GP on their wine sales is usually higher than on their food, but it's those salty Spanish nibbles and exotic-looking sharing platters that are the lure. And just as hand-raised pork pie, farmhouse Cheddar and assorted home-made pickles are staples of the otherwise food-free micropub, so tapas or its equivalent – cheese, charcuterie and olives – is pretty much the ideal food for the small wine bar owner. There are many wholesalers up and down the country who sell ready-made tapas and canapés of excellent quality as well as genuine imported cheeses, cold meats and so forth, so the amount of time and effort you have to put into prepping is very nearly zero. That not only makes the food cost efficient, it also makes the service potentially very quick, which (depending on your location) will underpin a viable lunchtime trade.

In the evenings you can run both hot and cold buffets majoring on sharing platters for serious diners but also offering impulse-driven, inexpensive, small plates for drinking patrons suffering attacks of the munchies. Tapas in particular create an opening for sherry and other Iberian fortified wines that in turn open the door to tasting nights, food and sherry matching events and other profitable promotions. You can keep up the theme by carrying a range of Spanish bottled beers – not everyone likes wine, after all!

Tapas bars may be growing in popularity, and there are few British cities today that don't have a handful of them, but Spain is not the only country to specialise in luxury wines and impulsive snacks. In Italy small bars known as bàcari or osterie commonly serve cicchetti (or cicheti in Venice), which are snacks that, like tapas, can be scaled up to a full meal. The French, of course, have wines, spirits, beers, ciders, canapés, pâtés, terrines, cheeses, charcuterie, salads, marinated vegetables and breads in embarrassing profusion. And meze bars, taking their inspiration from Greece, Turkey, Lebanon, Syria and even North Africa, are also spreading across the country. (There used to be a British equivalent called savouries, generally handed out at cocktail parties or with the apéritifs but now seemingly extinct.) It's revealing that operations of this kind are more likely to be found in the high streets of residential suburbs than in city centres, and that review sites commonly score them as medium price with stays ranging from 45 minutes to two hours. These are indicators of the flexibility of tapas, meze, cicchetti and the like and consequently of the split personalities of the places that serve them as both bars and restaurants: a quick lunch; a casual bite and glass of wine before the cinema; a romantic and impressively sophisticated (he hopes) dinner for two on a none-too-generous budget. Or maybe a big happy noisy party round a big table virtually collapsing under the weight of Mediterranean nibbles. This is almost the perfect format for a wine-loving would-be bar owner faced with a derelict laundrette and limited capital.

Wine training

If you've come this far you probably know almost all there is to know about the wines you plan to sell. But if you feel it's time to turn a passion into a profession you will probably be ready for the Wine & Spirit Education Trust's Level 2 Award in Wine Service. The WSET runs courses at four levels at dozens of centres all over the country, delivered either as evening classes, day releases or block releases. Level 1 is probably too basic for you and costs £150–175 depending on location and delivery. Level 2 at £350–£425, again depending on method of delivery and location, is more likely to suit you, and below is a brief summary of the syllabus. Visit **www.wsetglobal.com** for more information.

- Wine Tasting: Taste and describe 30–35 wines using the

Fortified wines

Fortified wines carry a good GP and create a sophisticated atmosphere but are something of a hard sell these days. Nevertheless, they still have potential. Chilled fino in particular is definitely due a comeback if only as an integral part of a tapas offering (see above), and – who knows – it might even be rediscovered by hipsters?

More generally, fortified wines were once a middle-class standby, and few lounge bars were without a row of them – a ruby port, a fino, a medium amontillado, a cream sherry and maybe in a particularly classy old country inn a Madeira. Today – and perhaps the general disappearance of lounge bars has something to do with it – fortified wines other than port are something of a curiosity, and many pubs don't stock sherry at all, let alone Madeira. This is perhaps a missed opportunity because branded sherries such as Croft Original, Harveys Bristol Cream (both sweet), and Tio Pepe (very dry!) that cost £11–£12 wholesale will retail for £40–£45 (15x50ml or 10x70ml).

Still, there's no point carrying stock that just takes up space on the bar-back, gathering dust. There are ways to promote fortified wines: if you stock them they should be on your wine list; in the right neighbourhood and with the right clientele a Port and Sherry Club might bring in some custom on an otherwise quiet night; chilled fino is a feature of a tapas or seafood special, as we have seen; Sherry is also a component of a number of cocktails, many of them also involving vermouth. To make a cobbler, for instance, pour 50ml of soda over a teaspoonful of white caster sugar in a cocktail glass, stir to dissolve, half-fill the glass with crushed ice, add 50ml cream sherry, stir again and top with a maraschino cherry and a twist of citrus peel. An East Indian is simpler still: mix equal parts fino sherry and dry vermouth, add a dash of Angostura bitters, shake with ice and pour. Foolproof!

WSET Systematic Approach to Tasting.
- Food and Wine Matching: A guide to the key considerations when matching food and wine successfully.
- Wine Service and Storage: Learn the correct way to store and serve wine and recognise common faults.
- Labelling: Learn how to decode and understand labels.
- Factors influencing the Style of Wine: Study the factors influencing the style, quality and price of wine in the vineyard and winery.
- Grape Varieties: Learn about the styles of wines produced by the key grape varieties.
- Key Wine-Producing Regions: Learn about the main styles of wines from the key wine-producing regions – France, Germany, Italy, Spain, Portugal, USA, Argentina, Chile, Australia, New Zealand and South Africa.

A study pack consisting of the course book (*A Comprehensive Guide to the Wines of the World*), and a study guide complete with maps, example questions, forms for your own tasting notes and laminated tasting card are usually included. The course comprises 16 taught hours and 12 hours of additional private study, most of which should be completed beforehand. There's a one-hour exam with 50 multiple choice questions and a pass mark of 55 per cent.

Wine service

Despite its popularity and indeed its ubiquity, wine still has more cachet than beer, so as well as stocking a selection that's the best possible quality within your customers' price range, you need to store and serve it with due regard for its status, with a little solemnity, even with some theatricality. And if the old charade of showing the customer the label and offering him the cork to sniff is perhaps taking the theatricality a little too far these days, storage, temperature and glassware are still (as with beer) indispensable parts of the presentation.

With wine, display and storage are inseparable. Cases of wine can be stored anywhere cool and stable, but since you can go through a single bottle in three large servings you need at least a session's worth of replacement bottles of your quickest sellers immediately to hand. But remembering that wine sells strongly on image, you don't want straightforward shelves of facings like the wine aisle in a supermarket. Sufficient white wine for the session must, of course, be kept in a chiller cabinet; for your reds, racks of different kinds are practical and space-saving and can be both eye-catching and classy.

This is the perfect excuse for a nice bit of theatre that will help create interest and even excitement around your wine offering: a well-presented wine list, either formal or informal according to your customer base, and with brief descriptions and tasting notes for each, gives customers a chance to browse and engage. Don't get carried away with the notes: a few words will do. But don't be too terse, either. The words 'dry' and 'medium' by themselves convey almost nothing, while easily-intelligible descriptors such as 'floral', 'fruity' and 'aromatic' are both accurate and evocative. 'Buckets of mangoes' is probably best avoided.

The cork can be an additional piece of theatre. Most wine is sold in screwtops these days, so a deliberate preference for corked bottles puts a welcome distance between your wine and Tesco's. The wines may be identical in quality and price, but a cork has more cachet. Proper corks give men the chance to tell their partners knowingly that that's why your wines are stored in horizontal racks, because the corks mustn't be allowed to dry out: actually, your wine isn't on the premises for more than a week or two and even though it spends nearly all that time upright, the chances of the corks drying out are precisely nil. But it's a nice story. The process of drawing the cork, either with a waiter's friend or with a bar-mounted corkscrew, is another special little ritual you don't get with screwtops.

> **Opening Champagne**
>
> This is as good a juncture as any to supply precise instructions on the correct opening of Champagne and other sparkling wines. (1) The bottle should be well rested and at its correct serving temperature of 7°C. (2) Hold the bottle firmly and upright (health and safety gone completely sensible here) in one hand. (3) Grasp the cork firmly in the other hand and unscrew it without moving the bottle. (4) The cork will come free with a disappointingly quiet 'pop' and can be removed gently, cleanly and without showering your customers with sticky fizz. Sparkling wines should be trickled down the (in)side of a glass held at an angle, just like lager, as this prevents overfoaming, wastage and mess. Still wines, by contrast, should be poured confidently into the centre of a level glass and snapped back upright smartly when the correct measure is poured (leaving plenty of headspace for swirling and nosing, as you'll doubtless be aware). This prevents drips staining your crisp white tablecloth.

Glassware for wines

Glassware is essential to the serve. Generations ago the norm in uncouth Britain was the round-bowled Paris goblet, which is really a miniature Burgundy glass, filled to the brim and holding about 120ml without spilling. Spirits were often served in the same style of glass. But wine lovers pointed out correctly that to get the best out of your wine the glass needed plenty of headspace in which the aromatic vapours could collect; and when celebrity wine critics started appearing on TV advocating the much bigger Bordeaux glass, the fate of the parsimonious little Paris goblet was sealed. Ordinary folk, though, didn't get the accompanying message that the whole point of the bigger glass was its headspace, not its capacity. Consumers who didn't drink with their noses objected to being served 125ml in a glass that would actually hold 300ml; insensibly the standard measure crept up to 175ml; and in time the monstrous measure of 250ml – a third of a bottle! – appeared as well.

There are – this being a topic closely connected with France – a plethora of 'correct' wine glasses to choose from and ferocious arguments about which of them is actually correct and which is vilest heresy. Every style, as with Belgian beer, has its shape. But while the sommelier of a Michelin-starred restaurant might rather eat his own feet than serve a Chablis in a Viognier glass, for the generic British publican there are only three wine glasses that really matter, the Bordeaux glass for table wines, the flute for sparkling wines and the good old Paris goblet for fortified wines. You will undoubtedly be a little more sophisticated than that: you wouldn't dream of serving sherry in anything but a copita, but don't go mad. Storage is one consideration: how many of each variety can you realistically stock? Imagine the embarrassment if you ran out of flutes and had to serve Prosecco in a dessert wine glass!

As with beer glasses, wine glasses must bear either a Crown stamp or a CE mark, and must be lined at 125ml and 175ml. (This isn't entirely true: if you sell wine by the bottle the glasses don't have to be stamped, and in restaurants where bottle sales are the norm they often aren't, but as you'll get all your glassware from the same supplier it might as well all be stamped.) The legal measures for table wine served by the glass are 125ml or 175ml, as above, or multiples of either; you have to have the smaller size available; and you have to post easily visible notices stating what measures you serve. Carafes are regulated too: they can be 25cl, 50cl, 75cl or 1l; but there's no legal measure for sparkling wines. Fortified wines may be served at 50ml or 70ml or multiples thereof. For more details Google the 1985 Weights & Measures Act.

Case study
1855 Wine Bar, Oxford

Opened in 2013 but named after the year in which the great vineyards of Bordeaux were officially classified, 1855 is the perfect example of a new wave of British wine bars that appeal, unlike their ancestor, to a younger breed of urban sophisticates. Wine – good wine, that is – is the serious side of hip. To know at least enough about it to order with confidence shows style and class, and to be able to order from the foot of the list without going pale and feeling faint is a sign that the purchaser has arrived. But with wine it's not all show: the quality is real and so is the pleasure.

It was love of wine pure and simple that drove founder Chris Mulhall – a nuclear physicist by trade – to open 1855 in a unit in Oxford's ancient and extremely attractive Castle complex that had previously been a Krispy Kreme doughnut franchise. "I'd studied wine for years, but only as an enthusiastic amateur," he says. "I was actually on a skiing holiday in California and fitting in some tastings in 2012 when it came to me that I really wanted a new career in the wine trade. Something like a wine bar, in fact. This unit gave me pretty much a blank canvas, and I was inspired by modern wine bars such as Vinoteca where the wine is taken very, very seriously. It's been getting harder and harder to find eclectic and original wines because the big shippers have been concentrating on margin and the market has been flooding with very undistinguished mass-produced wines, some of which are hardly drinkable. But there is something of a resurgence happening now, especially in European wines produced by small growers, and by working closely with independent shippers I've been able to source some really interesting ones, especially sustainable, natural, organic and biodynamic wines."

Alongside a selection of mainly but by no means entirely European wines ranging from a modest £20.70 up to no more than the mid-30s, there's a small but imaginative charcuterie 'n' cheese menu, including such cosmopolitan delicacies as duck rillettes, with small plates starting at £4 and boards from £10.95–£12.95. "This is a wine bar that serves food," says Chris. "Most of our wines are available by the glass. You don't have to order a meal to drink here, and as we don't have a huge kitchen our menu is necessarily limited."

Oxford is, Chris admits, exactly the right city for a venture like 1855. The Castle is a secondary location some 460m (1,500ft) from the city centre and some way off the main tourist drag, which allows 1855 an atmosphere of seclusion and exclusivity without having to charge exorbitantly, rents here being somewhat lower than in the centre proper. "I can get away with a GP of 70% on most wines, provided I am supplying an unusual and original list that customers will actually seek out," Chris concludes.

Finally, a minor headache for anyone who sells wine by the glass is how to preserve the contents of opened bottles. There are many gas-flushing and other devices on the market such as Coravin, Vacuvin and Winesave, and all very useful for wine buffs who might want to keep an opened bottle of a particularly special wine for three or even four days. If, on the other hand, you find that it takes that long to sell some of your more expensive wines, then just stop stocking them. Having said all that, there will always be one or two opened bottles left over almost every night. Just stopper them up securely and put them out of the way: they'll suffer no harm. But if they don't sell next day, either drink them yourself or donate them to the kitchen.

Wine on tap

Bag-in-box packaging was invented in Australia in 1965 and enables you to serve glass after glass (or carafe after carafe) in as-fresh condition and at the optimum temperature. It is also a great way of saving bar-back space while reducing waste to zero. And yet as late as 2015 it only accounted for 1 per cent of value sales in the UK on-trade.

The reason has been a lingering public perception of bag-in-box wine as representing value in the take-home trade and therefore not as classy as wine from the bottle, even if it's exactly the same liquid and the plastic bag from which it's dispensed is every bit as inert as glass. However, this perception has been gradually changing for a long time. Neither the Ladies Who Lunch or the Women's Night Out crowd or any other by-the-glass or carafe customers want to be shown the label and given the cork to sniff. They want four regular cab sauvs (or 10 large Chardonnays) and they want them now. From the licensee's point of view the 10l bag-in-box draught option is the perfect way of serving this increasing proportion of by-the-glass wine consumers as quickly and efficiently as humanly possible. You don't have to open a fresh container

Temperature

Serving temperature is always a tricky one with bottled wine (although not so with draught). A connoisseur will tell you that every style has its own ideal temperature and that red wine should be opened to breathe half an hour before pouring. A modern revisionist will tell you that it's all nonsense and red wines can even be served lightly chilled. This is all fine for the dinner-party host managing three or four different wines at most over the course of a leisurely evening and able to fuss and fidget over minute variations in temperature. As a busy bar owner all you need to know is this: red wines 12–18°C, still white wines (including dry sherry) 8–12°C; Champagne and other sparklers 5–7°C. If your cellar or the cupboard under your stairs or wherever it is that you keep your wine isn't particularly cold, then every morning, an hour or so before opening, transfer enough white and sparkling wines to the chiller cabinet and enough red to the ambient-temperature racks behind the bar to last the whole day's service.

every three or four serves, you don't have to stock mountains of bottles, there are no fiddly corkscrews, shelf-life is vastly prolonged and there are no breakages.

A very astute decision to serve the screamingly popular Prosecco on draught, although for some reason it annoyed the Italians, gave draught wines a place in the front row and prompted the industry to move towards supplying quite superior wines as bag-in-box. As a result of that, optimistic forecasters predicted that wine on tap could reach 15 per cent of on-trade value sales by 2020. But now there's a new development that looks likely to accelerate the growth of draught wines still further.

Wine kegs, holding 32 bottles each, are a conscious adaptation of KeyKeg technology. Inside a rigid airtight cylinder there's a heavy-duty recyclable plastic bag; compressed air is fed into the outer, squeezing the liquid out of the bag and straight into the carafe or glass. Importer Borough Wines says the wine keg's savings in terms of packaging, transport and ease of service make it possible to fill better-quality wines without putting prices up. Wine kegs also have the cachet of eco-friendliness, and the fact that the bags themselves are strictly one-way, even if they are recyclable, is offset by the fact that don't have to be cleaned with corrosive pollutants.

The Wine Producers Handbook

A practical guide to setting up a vineyard and winery in the UK

Belinda Kemp & Emma Rice

- FREE COPY OF THE VINEYARDS MAP OF ENGLAND AND WALES
- The most comprehensive and up-to-date guide on the market
- Written by Belinda Kemp, (Brock University Cool Climate Oenology and Viticulture Institute) and Emma Rice, Director of Wine at Hattingley Valley
- The essential commercial and business manual for potential vineyard owners and winemakers in UK
- Packed with anecdotes and case studies of people who have set up their own vineyards in UK
- Directories of useful websites, government regulations, vineyards, service providers and equipment manufacturers
- Now in its second edition and completely updated and revised
- **£12.95 plus postage and packing**

www.posthousepublishing.com

07

Café and bars

Trading all day: breakfast	161
Morning coffee and brunch	162
Lunch	162
Afternoon tea	164
Coffee	165
Tea and chocolate	168
Soft drinks	169

Case Study
Loungers, Bristol — *170*

Britain has a history of unlicensed cafés selling breakfast and lunch to working people dating back to the temperance crusades of the late 19th century. Their descendants are still a common feature of our high streets, but in recent years an increasing number of them – in many cases under the ownership of Greek and Turkish proprietors who see nothing odd about cafés that also sell beer – have obtained liquor licences. For many of them the ability to sell cans or bottles of lager has meant nothing more than a new line with a good margin. For others, the availability of alcohol has led to a deeper shift in their pattern of sales, taking the emphasis off the breakfast trade when there's no demand for beer and laying it instead on a new-found evening clientele.

From this there has emerged a new kind of bar that is superficially similar to the micropub: a small(ish) shop premises in a secondary location, at a low rent and therefore paying low or even no business rates, and negligible utilities and insurance, but with a very different style and scale of operation. The difference is mainly one of ambition, but it is very profound. The micropub owner is typically a cask beer devotee hoping to make a decent living but motivated primarily by lifestyle rather than money, and certainly not planning to work himself or herself to death or develop a large and complex business. This usually manifests itself through limited opening hours and vanishingly low overheads.

The café bar proprietor is exactly the opposite: with an entrepreneur's eye, he or she sees an unpromising venue with hidden potential that can only be revealed by a versatile and flexible approach to trade. This manifests itself by an urge to sweat every cover as efficiently as possible throughout a day that starts at breakfast and goes on until mid or even late evening. But it's impossible for an owner-operating couple to run a six-day two-shift business on their own, so unlike the micropub the café bar's GP has to cover a wage bill. And that means that someone's got to be up with the lark to dole out the Full English breakfasts.

Trading all day: breakfast

Until a decade or so ago, a café fry-up at breakfast time was typically the domain of labourers whose day started early and who often left home before the rest of the family were up. But as chain coffee shops became more and more common, so did the habit of picking up a large cappuccino and maybe a croissant to take to the office. Location was important too: high street and railway station sites were overwhelmingly the most successful.

Since then, breakfast has become an established part of the eating-out market, and it's not only made up of early-bird builders and nine-to-fivers grabbing a coffee and a pastry on their way into work. An increasing number of office workers are leaving home early to give themselves time for a leisurely breakfast, without having to cook or even pour a bowl of cereal, somewhere near the station or the office. A surprising number of parents stop on their way to or from school, too, to give their children a decent breakfast or to stop for a coffee and a bit of peace on the way back. And then there are older people with time on their hands who sometimes fancy a luxury breakfast they haven't had to make for themselves (or wash up after). In one 2015 survey 37 per cent of respondents said they ate breakfast out either regularly or at least from time to time, and the trend is upwards.

A very useful tip here from a pub that branched out into the breakfast trade with considerable success is to take the opportunity to get regular breakfast customers to place and pay for their lunchtime sandwich order at the same time. The advantage to them is that all they have to do is turn up and collect it; the advantage to you is that the quicker the lunchtime service the more lunches you can sell. Make sure they order a soft drink at the same time: the margin is enormous!

Morning coffee and brunch

Over the same period, as daily timetables have become less rigid the traditional modest mid-morning elevenses has been joined by brunch, and now 24 per cent of us confess to enjoying a little or not-so-little something at 11.00 am or thereabouts. The mid-morning crowd has a distinct identity and again, as with late breakfast, the demand is more for the leisurely than the rushed. Tourists taking a break from sightseeing; mums with pushchairs taking a break from their routines; shoppers taking a break from shopping; pensioners just taking a break. Chain-owned coffee shops may have captured most of this trade, but the owner-operated café bar has an advantage in its scope for individuality. You're not obliged to stock whatever stale mass-produced cake the franchise owner forces on you, nor pay above market price for it. Find a local patissier – and they really are everywhere – to create the very finest pastries and confections exclusively for you. Do that and make coffee more quickly that Starbucks or Costa do, and provided you can last out the awareness-building period you'll find in time that your morning session is populated by regulars exactly as your evening session is.

Lunch

It is an eternal, but from the caterer's point of view most pleasing, mystery of British culture that shop and office workers so rarely take their lunches to work with them. Factory workers and miners used to, when there were such beings, but the white-collar workforce prefers to splash out on a sandwich that will cost them ten times what it would if they made it themselves. Today's high street, therefore, has myriad concerns fighting for that sandwich, and you are well placed to compete successfully with the best of them.

There are, in essence, two lunchtime markets: quick counter service of both eat in and take out orders, and cook-to-order customers. They are both definitely worth fighting for: cook-to-order has a slow rate of sale but a high spend per head; counter service has a lower spend per head but a lightning rate of sale. With a carefully planned menu, cook-to-order doesn't necessarily involve that much more time and labour, and the extra cost can be clawed back by drinks sales. The key to success in both of them is quick service: many office workers these days don't get a full hour, and tourists and shoppers who have all the time in the world have learned to be impatient. And the key to quick service is preparation, both of counter service and cook-to-order items.

Counter service items can all be prepared in advance. During the morning when you're preparing the advance orders placed at breakfast-time you can also be filling the sandwiches, rolls, baguettes and wraps for your chiller cabinet. Ham and cheese, with or without tomato and/or relishes, are still Britain's best-selling fillings, but you can also cook up more sausages, eggs (boiled and fried) and bacon at breakfast than you need and make sarnies with them at a very low cost. You can afford to try more adventurous fillings than the competition, too: if no-one buys the half-dozen Hungarian salami and pesto on rye you made, you can always eat them yourself; it will have cost you very little and you'll have learned an awful lot. In fact, why not be the first lunch counter on your block to have a suggestions box? You can also load up a chiller with bought-in pies and pasties and a selection of more exotic delicacies from wholesale catering suppliers, most of whom these days can supply good-quality ranges of tapas, meze, sushi, charcuterie and other deli delights at reasonable prices. You can also fill up an electric soup-kettle (a 10-litre one in a rather appealing cast iron-effect finish costs less than £60 + VAT) and serve the soup in mugs, not bowls: more eye-catching and much harder to spill.

The important point here is that, as with the Hungarian salami and pesto on rye, you can experiment cheaply in small batches, discover what your customers will go for that the competition doesn't already sell and create yourself a locally unique profile. (Hungarian salami on rye is delicious, by the way, but probably not with pesto.) A couple more tips to help mark you out: use better bread than the neighbouring sandwich shops and never ever use margarine! (However, do keep a tub of synthetic spread on hand for vegan and lactose-intolerant customers, and advertise on the sandwich menu that it's an option.) And finally, more of a general point than lunchtime-specific: count the cost of every single item, however small. How much is that jar of chutney and how many sandwiches did it make? How many slices to a loaf of bread? You have to obsess over this, and you have to be damned sure that every single consumable in the place down to the last sugar cube makes at least 100 per cent and preferably 120 per cent.

Afternoon tea

In urban bars the lunchtime service may ease off from 2.30 pm but it's usually still possible to trade through the afternoon. Trade at cafés also dies off after lunch as demand for substantial meals and savouries dwindles, but coffee shops are still hard at work catering to a very similar demand to the one that keeps them busy in the morning. Some 23 per cent of us confess to eating out between 3.00–6.00 pm and again it's mainly shoppers, tourists and the elderly doing the spending with tea, coffee, biscuits and cakes being the preferred items. Scones with clotted cream and strawberry jam seem particularly irresistible. If you've captured some of the morning trade from chain coffee shops and mall cafés, then there's no reason why you shouldn't be just as successful in the afternoons, especially in summer when you can turn your pavement tables into an outdoor gelateria, which many of your franchised competitors won't have the facilities for.

(And even if they do, you can source better ice-cream than they can.)

Building up a viable afternoon trade may be less straightforward in suburbs and villages than in high streets, but if you're anywhere near a school you may well get a 3.30 pm boost from parents who for perfectly good reasons – they may be single or working parents who are both time-poor and by this time of day utterly exhausted – would rather buy their kids' tea in a café than have to make it themselves. Put on a typical kids' menu of easy-to-prepare items such as fish fingers and baked beans and you'll find that even at a low retail price there's a good margin. And it's not just the fact that you're doing both the cooking and the washing-up that parents will welcome but also the opportunity for half an hour's peace with a cuppa and a cake and a bit of networking with others in a similar situation. You might even lay in a few small items of play equipment or diversions such as colouring books. The demand for this sort of facility is there, especially in villages and suburbs where everything else has closed down, and it's a demand you are ideally placed to fulfil.

Coffee

You're a café bar. You have to have coffee. You have to have good coffee, too – in fact you have to have the best coffee in the high street. And not just to attract customers, but because of this one fact: a cup of good-quality cafétière coffee can be made for as little as 12p. It can be sold at £2, a profit margin that comfortably exceeds anything else you'll ever sell. But it does far more than that. If it's really good coffee (and instant should never, ever, ever be allowed through your door), sold confidently and positively, it can be used to lever open several hours' extra trading a day. Good coffee entices people in for breakfast. Good coffee with cake entices people in for elevenses. Good coffee entices Mums With Pushchairs in for afternoon coffee, with yet more cake. (See below for tea!)

Britain's gone a bit mad for a market sector that didn't even exist 20 years ago, and its growth has depended to a large extent on the quality of the product. Before branded coffee shops started spreading across the country's high streets like a rash, cafés were places where you could get round-the-clock bacon, sausages and beans washed down by mugs of builder's tea or watery, insipid instant coffee. Even genteel tearooms that did tea and scones really well could only run to watery, insipid instant coffee; and you knew you were home from your holiday in France when you stopped for a coffee at a motorway service station and yes, it was watery, insipid and instant.

Yet in 2015, British consumers got through 70 million cups of out-of-home coffee a day and paid £730 billion for them, or more than £2 each. Branded chains and independents accounted for about 30 per cent of that each, while the remaining 40 per cent was mopped up by non-specialists including pubs, restaurants and hotel bars. So here is a very profitable sector in which you can compete as strongly as anyone, and the key to competing here is good-quality beans. The branded chains have created high expectations that competitors have to outmatch. You'll find a list and a map of over 300 independent suppliers spread all over the UK at **www.thecoffeeroasters.co.uk**: any one of them will supply you their own standard blends or create a unique customised range just for you – at a cost, of course – but given the margins, not all that much of a cost.

After the beans, the method of preparation, and those huge, hissy, dramatic espresso machines you see in branded coffee shops are almost certainly out of the question. Even to lease they cost a fortune; they take up far too much space; and they require a lot of staff. Worse than that, they take forever to produce a tiny cup of coffee – and if queuing is all part of the experience at a Starbucks or Costa, it doesn't work in a quick-service lunch counter. The other options, which all have the space-saving advantage of being hidden away in the kitchen, are:

- Individual cafétières – easy to prepare behind the scenes; zero waiting time if you have a kettle-tap or even a humble urn; the customers get to decide how strong they have their coffee; nice presentation; about 12p a cup. On the downside it's Americano or nothing.
- Individual filter pots – again, easy to prepare, zero waiting time and nice presentation, but the range of options is equally limited and they can seem to drip forever. About 15p a cup.
- Single-serve pods – quick, easy and versatile. Not very environmentally friendly, though, and you have no control over the quality of the beans themselves. Expensive at 40–45p a cup.
- Bean-to-cup machines – produce an espresso base suitable for Americanos, lattés, cappuccinos etc.; available in commercial sizes that can make 200 cups a day; will grind the beans, make the coffee and dispense it automatically with minimal supervision. Can be expensive to lease, and as ever the leases have to be professionally checked! About 22p a cup.

Having selected your format you can choose the level of presentational flourish to suit: cute little jugs and even metal nanochurns for the milk; complimentary biscotti or chocolates; rough-cut sugar cubes or even sugar swizzle sticks. And if you're buying your coffee from a local roaster and the customers like it, you can make a little extra by stocking bags for sale.

Finally, you can make your coffee offering stand out – particularly after meals – by reviving a few formats from the past. Liqueur coffees from the 1970s are making something of a comeback in an ironic Abigail's Party/Berni Inn kind of way; but who remembers café crème as it used to be – strong black coffee with a silky layer of single cream on top, poured slowly over the back of a cold spoon to stop it sinking? And then there's percolated coffee, ostracised for years because of the effects of letting it boil and the violence inflicted on the grounds by the constant circulation of the hot water. It's big, rough, tough stuff: it's the kind of coffee favoured by John Wayne on a 1,000-mile cattle drive; it's close in spirit to Greek and Turkish coffee; it sorts out the men from the boys.

Tea and chocolate

About tea there is little to be said except that even if you use teabags instead of leaf, it should always be properly brewed and served in pots; that there's a staggering range available; that it keeps well in a cool dark place, so that you can afford to maintain a small stock of speciality teas for which you have only slow demand; and that its margin is just as high as coffee's. And it's another area where your serve can be luxuriously posh without adding a penny to your overhead: good tea, nice china, cream as an option; and, to add a little to the spend, well-made scones, superior jam, and whipped or clotted cream as well as your usual range of posh cakes. Luxurious, sophisticated, sinful, but at value for money that makes it virtuous.

Hot chocolate, perhaps surprisingly, outsells tea in the licensed trade. Powdered hot chocolate from a tin, with a squirt of tinned whipped cream and a marshmallow on top is a great indulgence in winter, and kids love it all year round. It's terribly quick and easy to make, especially if you heat the milk in the microwave rather than on the hob (or buy a brand with the milk powder already added), and as the ingredients cost next to nothing the profit margin can be very good.

For the dining room there's a luxury alternative that will

make diners feel really spoilt: simply melt four squares (or more) of good quality dark chocolate slowly in hot but never boiling full-fat milk with a level teaspoon of rich muscovado sugar; let it cool slightly; pour; stir in a couple of teaspoons of single cream; and finally top with a float of whipped cream or Chantilly. That'll cost you less than a pound and is worth a fiver of anybody's money.

Soft drinks

With a gross profit of 300 – 400 per cent, soft drinks have always been a significant contributor to positive cash flow; and developments over the last half-century have seen that contribution grow. Breath-testing since the 1960s, the inexorable rise of the family trade and increasing health and weight consciousness have all given margin-rich soft drinks a large and welcome presence. This in turn has stimulated innovation among makers, transforming what used to be a largely generic market into one of premium brands with commensurately premium pricing: 2015–16 saw overall on-trade soft drink sales rise 0.9 per cent in volume but 4.4 per cent in value to £4.3 billion. But a large part of the market's strength stems from its variety, creating the familiar challenge of market segmentation and category management – of satisfying as many demands as possible given the available space.

The basic carbonates – cola, tonic and lemonade in both diet and regular versions – are still by far the biggest category with over 40 per cent of market volume, and despite the huge sums spent by the two leading colas on branding they can all be treated pretty much as generic and served on draught. To these should be added a budget ginger beer, which is becoming more and more popular because of its versatility but at the time of writing doesn't appear to be available in syrup or concentrate form. Alongside the basic carbonates are those other good old standbys, the sticky

Case Study
Loungers, Bristol

With the pub trade in its deepest crisis for a century, the quest to reinvent the local - to give customers a reason for abandoning their cinema-sized HDTVs and computer games - is a daily struggle. Perhaps the pub's successor is somewhere as buzzy and bright as a really lively local but without the historic trappings that tend to make some people feel excluded. Somewhere you can casually drop in and out of, with or without kids and pushchairs and shopping bags, somewhere you can have anything from coffee and a cake to a full three-course meal with wine - in short, a café-bar. These are nothing new, of course, but the Lounger concept is quite different from the branded city-centre café-bars of 20 years ago. Launched in 2002, it's the brainchild of partners Alex Reilley, Jake Bishop and Dave Reid who had all trained in restaurants in Bristol and, significantly, had no experience whatsoever of the pub trade.

Loungers was inspired by bars in Australia and New Zealand as an all-day concept with a relaxed and informal approach to the menu and service, neither a pub nor a restaurant, with as broad an appeal as possible. "We didn't really have a grand plan," says Alex. "We just wanted the sort of place we'd go into ourselves." Hardly a revolutionary model, albeit a rather exotic one!

The first branch was a former optician's shop in the Bristol suburb of Southill, an area that was gentrifying as the property boom drove young professionals out of the more desirable areas of the city centre but had yet to develop the kind of social facilities they were used to. So despite being tiny - it only had room for 10 tables - it met a need among the new inhabitants not just for blokey tapas and beer in the evening but also for young families during the day. And as a shop conversion that shoppers and office-workers saw as a café rather than a pub, it had none of the identifiers that often deter casual drop-ins, while its location on a secondary high street meant there were plenty of passers-by.

"People there were desperate for the sort of things you expect of metropolitan life – like a decent cup of coffee, for example," says Alex. That also meant stocking upmarket brands such as Fentimans and Pago soft drinks and Westons and Orchard Pig ciders as well as a small but well-chosen range of cask ales, superior spirits, decent wines and cocktails – the sort of comforts that young professionals want and expect. But if it was adult-oriented it was also very family-friendly, and soon it became a mixture of local pub, social club and village hall not just for incomers but for people with local roots as well; and some customers were visiting two or three times a day – late breakfast at 9.00 am, then a light lunch followed by a proper evening out.

"We didn't have huge expectations, so we were pleasantly surprised to find that so many people shared our idea of what would be a nice place to use, and we soon realised that the key market was within a mile radius," says Alex. A local drop-in, then, where – not to overemphasise the concept's Antipodean roots – good neighbours could become good friends. Just what the old-fashioned local aspired to be, but with added women and kids.

The chain has expanded dramatically in its 15 years and at the time of writing has 87 branches, mostly in the high streets of suburbs like Southill that are evolving into 'quarters', and mostly in cities in the south-west and West Midlands. Not one of them has ever been a pub. They don't look like pubs, and they don't operate like pubs either, but they fulfil the same role that pubs have always done in their communities. Food makes up 50 per cent of turnover and coffee makes up a healthy 11 per cent. The branches are busy throughout the day, but 55 per cent of the takings come after 4.00 pm. There are a further 20 Cosy Clubs, similar in inspiration but rather larger and grander.

Perhaps for operators seeking to revive the fortunes of the local, Loungers are the model to emulate. They have succeeded by stripping away some of the more forbidding aspects of the traditional pub: the big clear-glass windows – pioneered, it should be acknowledged, by All Bar One – are obviously more welcoming than frosted and etched glass, however historic. In from-scratch conversions there are no issues with access for the disabled. At certain times of day kids – and buggies and pushchairs – are everywhere, not merely tolerated as in a pub but firmly – umbilically, one might almost say – attached to the core clientele. And there's none of the air of fusty misogyny that still pervades all too many old-fashioned pubs.

It's all very well putting up a big poster that says 'all welcome', but locating and designing a site that turns a hopeful slogan into an effective operating model is a different matter altogether, and something that Loungers seems to have achieved almost by accident. "The term 'café-bar' has been one of the most misused expressions ever," says Alex. "All Bar One was the pioneer but it fell into the trap of narrowing its appeal to a certain category of consumer. But that's what Loungers are: they're cafés, and they're bars." So perhaps the pub of the future won't look like a pub, but it'll act like one. And the main difference between the new local and the old is that the new local doesn't stand on its dignity as the Great British Pub. It opens its eyes, finds the real demand – and nails it.

bottles of orange, blackcurrant and lime squash or cordial. These don't have to be branded and indeed look their best in matching carafes. If you keep them on their own salver on the bar-back you save space, make a little feature of them and stop sticky drips getting everywhere, and make sure they're always to hand (they usually seem to wander somehow). You might also add a fourth to the trinity: peppermint cordial. Whether you charge for these is up to you: the customer probably won't notice, but over time your bottom line will.

How varied and extended your range is depends on how much weight you put on the largely female daytime trade. Women will form the largest category of soft drink consumers unless your bar is absolutely overrun with under-18s, which seems unlikely somehow. As a market segment, women drink less alcohol than men: in an Office of National Statistics survey 52 per cent of women said they had consumed alcohol during the preceding week compared with 64 per cent of men, and 25 per cent of women said they were teetotal compared with 18 per cent of men; 7 per cent of women admit to regularly exceeding the Health Department guidelines compared with 11 per cent of men. And when women do drink alcohol, it's often combined with a soft drink or mixer in a long drink such as white wine spritzer, Amaretto and Coke, or Malibu and pineapple.

Women in general are also more health and weight conscious than men and try to consume less sugar. In this they have made a huge contribution to the rise of diet versions, which according to the British Soft Drinks Association's 2015 report accounted for 75 per cent of squashes and cordials and 49 per cent of carbonates. Pure fruit juice sales had suffered a decline, said the BSDA, because of their relatively high sugar content. When the sugar tax came into force in April 2018, this added up to 24p a litre to the price of the most sugary drinks, these percentages are expected to rise still further despite continuing concerns over the long-term health effects of the most common artificial sweetener, Aspartame.

It would be almost criminally negligent not to seize on such a good opportunity to increase repeat custom profitably by assembling a soft drink offering that is going to engage your female clientele. For a start, as we have seen, the margin on soft drinks is excellent and women are great traffic-builders. It's a truism in the trade that where women go, men follow, either as suitors or, later on in life, as husbands and fathers. A venue with a reputation for great girls' nights out will attract a plume of hopeful boys too; and another category of female customers you want to attract has the potential to make or break your daytime sessions: professional and/or well-to-do women who like to network or socialise in a relaxed and informal atmosphere – in short, Ladies Who Lunch.

Something that most women share is the sensitivity of their palates. As any brewer, parfumier or tea blender will tell you, women by and large have keener sense perceptions and more accurate sense memories than men, which is why they're in such high demand as tasters. They might make do with the standard offering, but their palates are attuned to much more sophisticated flavours. And to become their regular rendezvous you ought to offer them more than something they will merely make do with but something much classier – and especially something that makes them feel they are being looked after as women, not as adjuncts to men.

Fortunately the manufacturers are falling over themselves to present you with an arsenal of flavours and styles that will enable you to do just that. Just about every corner of Britain now has its artisan soft drinks maker whose list of ingredients sounds like the botanicals for a craft gin, and if you can't find one locally then nationally distributed brands like Fentimans and Bottle Green come in flavours including rose, lime and jasmine, elderflower (lots of elderflower!), mandarin and Seville orange, pomegranate (and elderflower), raspberry and grapefruit, mango and coconut, mint, apple, plum, cranberry, grapefruit, honeysuckle… the margin will make you annoyed that people will persist in drinking beer!

You can also, if you wish to be more adventurous still, make your own mocktails, which are simply cocktails – you've guessed it – without the alcohol. But the alcohol is all that's missing: the shaking and stirring and sparklers and umbrellas and theatricality and fun are all there – and so is the premium. There are a million recipes on the internet, and there's even a company now offering completely kosher alcohol-free spirits. Seedlip uses the simple distillation method universal among the apothecaries, herbalists and alchemists of old and still routinely practised by parfumiers today. Aromatic plant material – herbs, spices, flowers etc. – is either seethed or steamed with water in a pot-still; the vapour comprising steam and essential oils is collected and cooled; the flavoursome oils naturally rise to the top as the different vapours condense and can easily be separated for compounding. An inspired gimmick and a wonderful base for any mocktail!

Needless to say, these drinks are also the perfect offering for teetotallers, who make up a fifth of the adult population but often feel like afterthoughts in a licensed bar: tolerated, but expected to put up with sweet fruit-based carbonates. Make a teetotaller, whether male or female, a blackcurrant and sour apple daiquiri, with a bit of a chat as you mix it, and make them feel loved.

08

Food

Training	178
Hygiene	181
Environmental health inspections	185
Health and safety in the kitchen	186
Kitchen design and equipment	188
Waste disposal	190
Food without cooking	193

Case Study
Treacle Tap, Macclesfield *194*

Bearing in mind that the starting point of this book was turning small shop premises into successful bars, food service will probably not be uppermost in the minds of most readers. Most micropubs serve nothing more than bag snacks and in some cases light nibbles such as the licensee's home-made Scotch eggs. Others will rent or lend crockery and cutlery to customers who bring in takeaways. Many cocktail bars don't do much by way of food either: in both of these kinds of operations the drink is the star attraction. Wine bars and café bars are, of course, much more food-oriented but even here, as we've seen, there's no need for a particularly sophisticated kitchen or a highly skilled brigade de cuisine. But just as when you're starting a 20 x 20ft micropub you have to go through the same planning and licensing procedures as the new 100-bed Premier Inn being built down the road, so it is with food service. Gordon Ramsay and a couple running a lunch counter at a café bar bear the same burden of responsibility – i.e., not to poison the public – and are covered by much the same legislation.

Training

Escaping unpoisoned is not the only expectation your customers will have of you. The paying diner demands and has a right to food that lives up to its price tag, that is competently cooked (and tasty!) and that arrives within a reasonable time of being ordered. You don't have to be Gordon Ramsay to achieve this. What you do need, though, is an understanding based on experience of how different a commercial kitchen, however small, is from a domestic one and how different cooking for customers is from cooking for family and friends. Your culinary skills may be absolutely top-flight, but it's your managerial skill that matters when you have a queue of 17 office workers wanting nothing more complicated than a sandwich but wanting it right now. There's no substitute for experience, of course, and the best grounding in kitchen management is to start at the bottom.

But life can be so frenzied in a successful kitchen that you often have no alternative but to keep your head down and work without getting much of an idea of what's going on around you, so even at the lowest level of catering there is an important role for formal training as well.

You should start by downloading the Food Standards Agency's very helpful 40-page leaflet Starting Up: Your First Steps in Running a Catering Business from **www.food.gov.uk**. The leaflet doesn't set out to answer every question you might have, but it tells you what questions need answering. If that hasn't put you off, community colleges all over the country run very cheap part-time courses teaching knife skills and other such kitchen basics as well as the fundamentals of hygiene and health and safety for beginners. A one-day-a-week five-week course can cost as little as £115 at the time of writing (although prices vary from centre to centre). This might be just enough to get you started in the kitchen, but it's also a fairly quick and inexpensive way of making a useful kitchen-hand out of a willing novice.

Higher professional qualifications are provided by a great number of respected national institutions and are taught at local colleges and by private providers, all either full- or part-time, as well as online. Many of the syllabuses these institutions have developed cover broadly the same ground but with stronger emphases on specific areas. One of the most popular among budding chefs, for instance, is the Professional Cookery Level 2 Diploma from City and Guilds (**www.cityandguilds.co.uk**). This is pretty heavyweight stuff: the part-time course takes two full days a week, lasts for 35 weeks and will cost little short of £2,000. It's very food- and cookery-oriented, teaching you how to prepare and cook stocks, soups and sauces; fruit and vegetables; meat and offal; poultry; fish and shellfish; rice, pasta, grains and egg dishes; hot and cold desserts and puddings; pastry, biscuit, cake, sponge and bread. There are also modules on food safety, health and safety, operations, costs and menu planning, but unless you have very serious culinary ambitions you might be better advised to look at the more business-oriented British Institute of Innkeeping's Level 3 Award in Kitchen Management, taught at centres all over the country. This three-day course can cost anything from £200–£350 + VAT and packs in an amazingly broad syllabus under four headings:

- Managing People: Recruitment. Employee performance evaluations – preparation. Conducting an appraisal. Appraisal systems. Motivation. Identifying an unmotivated team. Re-motivating a team. Successful team-building. Managing people. Abuse and stress in kitchens. Conflict. Workforce planning. Building relationships between teams. New employees. Time management. Legislation and employee rights. Industrial tribunals.
- Managing Administration: Kitchen administration. Temperature recording. Stock ordering and control. Food cost. Gross profit. Profit and loss account. Labour as a percentage of sales. Menu descriptors. Incentive programmes. Kitchen meetings. Managing change.
- Managing the Kitchen Environment: Hazard Analysis Critical Control Points (HACCP). Risk assessments. Environmental health. Kitchen design and construction. Energy efficiency and carbon footprint.
- Managing Your Market: Competition. Marketing. SWOT analysis. Customer needs, wants and expectations. Identifying a target customer group. Categorising market segments. Customer occasions. Marketing objectives. Market and menu design. The marketing mix.

You might consider topping up your food hygiene and health and safety acumen by taking a Level 2 Food Safety in Catering award from the Chartered Institute of Environmental Health **www.cieh.org** as well; it can be taken at home or work for just north of £200.

Much of the above, especially the material dealt with under the first heading, is not really going to be all that relevant to the start-up owner-operator, but may well come in very handy as and when your business grows. Most of it, though, is invaluable: the ability to control your business can make the difference between success and failure.

Hygiene

One of the key themes in all of these courses is hygiene. The very last thing you want to do is give your customers food-poisoning, whether it be campylobacter, cholera, e. coli, hepatitis A, listeria, norovirus, rotavirus, staphylococcus, salmonella or indeed b. cereus, which is very cereus indeed and lives on cooked rice. Some of these pathogens are resistant to freezing, cooking and reheating, and some of them can be fatal. Okay, your kitchen is unlikely to be harbouring ciguatera, which originates from tropical fish, or shigellosis, which is caught from human faeces. But listeria is quite bad enough, thank you, and can be contracted from food as apparently innocent as cheese made from unpasteurised milk. And as any outbreak can land you in court and destroy your business's reputation for good, you want to take hygiene very seriously.

Since hygiene generally is one of the most heavily regulated areas in catering, it is highly recommended (although not actually a legal obligation) that you and your senior staff (if you have a large kitchen) should have Food Hygiene Certificates. Whether you regard the various acts, regulations and directives governing food safety as punitive regimes or helpful guidelines, there are an awful lot of them. The main ones are the Food Safety Act 1990, the Food Standards Act 1999, the General Food Regulations of 2004, EU

Allergen advice

Under the Food Information Regulations that came into force in 2014 service of all types of 'loose food' – a large category including all meals, hot or cold, not served in any sort of packaging – must be accompanied by allergen information. The Food Standards Agency, which is the regulating body, recognises 14 potentially dangerous allergens and it is your responsibility to ensure that customers are advised of which dishes contain which allergens.

There are two acceptable ways of transmitting the advice. The most thorough but probably least practical is to list allergens on the menu alongside any dish that contains them, e.g.: Chicken satay (contains peanuts). Alternatively, serving and waiting staff may advise customers as they order: if this is your preferred method you should say so on the menu and display a sign or signs to this effect. Staff should be able to give consistent and accurate information relating to each dish and there should be a further source of authoritative confirmation of the advice available to any customers with doubts or queries (i.e., you or your chef if you have one).

The 14 allergens are:
- Cereals containing gluten, namely wheat, spelt, rye, barley, oats and products thereof, except wheat-based glucose syrups including dextrose, wheat-based maltodextrins, glucose syrups based on barley and cereals used for making alcoholic distillates.
- Crustaceans and products thereof (for example prawns, lobster, crabs and crayfish).
- Egg and products thereof.
- Fish and products thereof, except fish gelatine used as carrier for vitamin or carotenoid preparations and fish

- gelatine or isinglass used as a fining agent in beer and wine.
- Peanuts and products thereof.
- Soybeans and products thereof, except fully refined soybean oil and fat, vegetable oils derived from soybean sources and plant stanol ester produced from vegetable oil sterols from soybean sources.
- Milk and products thereof (including lactose), except whey used for making alcoholic distillates including ethyl alcohol of agricultural origin and lactitol.
- Nuts (namely almond, hazelnut, walnut, cashew, pecan, Brazil, pistachio and macadamia) and products thereof except for nuts used for making alcoholic distillates.
- Celery and products thereof.
- Mustard and products thereof.
- Sesame seeds and products thereof.
- Sulphur dioxide and/or sulphites at concentrations of more than 10mg/kg or 10mg/L.
- Lupin and products thereof.
- Molluscs and products thereof (for example mussels, clams, oysters, scallops, snails and squid).

FIR is enforced by Environmental Health inspectors; breaches can be prosecuted and are punishable by a fine at the magistrates' discretion. For more detailed information visit **www.food.gov.uk** and look up the FSA's 20-page guide, updated in March 2017, Allergen Information for Loose Foods, and the even more detailed Food Allergen Labelling and Information Requirements.

Directive 178/2002, EU Directive 2073/2005, the Food Hygiene Regulations of 2006, the EU Food Information for Consumers Regulation of 2011 and the Food Hygiene Regulations of 2013 and 2015. You can Google them all if you have the time and patience, but they all boil down to much the same thing: don't make your customers ill. Or dead. And they are not to be taken lightly: there are no £60 spot fines and three points on your licence in the fight against food pathogens. In the days when summary offences (i.e. offences that could be tried by magistrates) carried a maximum fine of £5,000 or six months in prison, hygiene breaches were considered among the most serious. But in 2015 maximum summary fines were abolished, and you now face the possibility of an unlimited fine if you poison your customers. So get Food Hygiene Certificates for yourself and your senior staff – not only will the training make it less likely that you'll ever poison anyone, but if you do then possession of a certificate will help your defence by demonstrating your good intent.

City and Guilds Food Hygiene Certificate training courses are taught either part-time at FE colleges or online by private providers. Level 1 covers food safety awareness and is typically very cheap – one online provider charges just £10 + VAT. Level 2 is more practical and covers handling and preparation but is still cheap – £25 + VAT in the case of our sample provider. Level 3 is the course for managers and supervisors and will enable you to fulfil your legal obligation to supervise, instruct and train all food-handling staff. It's more expensive at £125 plus VAT but could be worth it depending on the size of your business. The Food Standards Agency **www.food.gov.uk** also has leaflets, videos and online material to help you train junior staff as well as three short but invaluable booklets, available on the same site as PDFs and intended for you: Food Hygiene – a Guide for Businesses; Starting Up – First Steps to Running a Catering Business; and Good Hygiene is Good for Business.

Environmental health inspections

You have to register as a food business with the district council's environmental health department at least 28 days before your opening date, and officers will then make a formal inspection to award you your stars – the so-called Scores on the Doors – under the Food Hygiene Recognition Standards scheme. The scheme was always intended to be carrot-led rather than stick-driven, but inevitably if you only have four stars to show off and not five, customers will be wondering which bit of the operation failed its inspection. And if you only have three you've got some work to do! If you don't agree with the assessment you have a right of appeal or (probably more constructively) you can ask for a reinspection once you've carried out any recommendations they might have made.

EHOs have an absolute right to inspect everything in your premises at any time during opening hours without so much as a by-your-leave, let alone an appointment, and they are notorious for arriving just when you're at your busiest. It's less and less likely in these straitened times that they're just dropping in on the off-chance: when they do show up then nine times out of ten they're following up a complaint. And they are very powerful people. They can slap you on the spot with a Hygiene Improvement Notice or a Food Labelling Notice requiring specified improvements to be carried out within a specified time, no argument and no foot-dragging allowed; and if your offence is more serious they can serve you with an Emergency Prohibition Notice or a Remedial Action Notice. Both entitle them to shut down part or all of your equipment and/or operation from condemning your ancient rust-covered extractor vent to closing the entire premises on the spot. The only difference is that the former has to be confirmed by a court (as does seizure and destruction of foods unfit for consumption), while the latter is instant. Finally, they can prosecute you; and as we've seen

Hygiene tips

Before the EHOs arrive for their first inspection, there's a fairly lengthy check-list of potential weaknesses to look for and deal with. The condition of the fabric and infrastructure is the most obvious: are there cracked or abraded surfaces or broken tiles in the floor, walls or ceiling? Is there any smell of drains (or drain unblocker)? Do taps run smoothly and do sinks drain quickly? Are any work surfaces damaged, and are they all wipe-down? Next, ease of maintenance and cleaning: are there odd nooks and crannies where dirt and grease might collect? Is it possible to clean underneath and behind all appliances? Can the upper surfaces of cupboards, shelving units, fridges, extractor hoods etc. be accessed easily? Are there enough hand basins? What system of hand-drying is provided? Where are the wastebins sited? Are there enough fridges? Next, the cooking appliances themselves: gas or electric? Ancient or modern? Try switching them on – do they actually work? Are there sufficient work-surfaces? Are they well-enough lit? Do they have conveniently-located cutlery drawers and knife blocks? And – critical, this – are there completely separate work-surfaces and chopping-boards for raw and cooked items?

Health and safety in the kitchen

Every commercial kitchen must be a safe place to work in and able to satisfy the 1974 Health and Safety at Work Act's opening clauses regarding the general duties of employers towards their staff, which are as follows:

(1) It shall be the duty of every employer to ensure, so far as is reasonably practicable, the health, safety and welfare at work of all employees.

(2) Without prejudice to the generality of an employer's duty under the preceding subsection, the matters to which that duty extends include in particular:

(a) the provision and maintenance of plant and systems of work that are, so far as is reasonably practicable, safe and without risks to health;

(b) arrangements for ensuring, so far as is reasonably practicable, safety and absence of risks to health in connection with the use, handling, storage and transport of articles and substances;

(c) the provision of such information, instruction, training and supervision as is necessary to ensure, so far as is reasonably practicable, the health and safety at work of employees;

(d) so far as is reasonably practicable as regards any place of work under the employer's control, the maintenance of it in a condition that is safe and without risks to health and the provision and maintenance of means of access to and egress from it that are safe and without such risks;

(e) the provision and maintenance of a working environment for employees that is, so far as is reasonably practicable, safe, without risks to health, and adequate as regards facilities and arrangements for their welfare at work.

(3) Except in such cases as may be prescribed, it shall be the duty of every employer to prepare and as often as may be appropriate revise a written statement of general policy with respect to the health and safety at work of employees and the organisation and arrangements for the time being in force for carrying out that policy, and to bring the statement and any revision of it to the notice of all employees.

The full text can be found at **www.legislation.gov.uk**, but be warned: with 85 provisions and 10 schedules it's a hefty piece of law. However, it's still well worth reading paragraphs 2–9, 18–25, 33–42 and 47 in their entirety. Some of them may be difficult to interpret, the legalese being as obfuscatory as it customarily is, but you will still come away understanding that this is serious legislation carrying serious penalties for transgression, and that it affects small kitchens just as much as huge ones.

Having said that, once you've studied the legislation itself rather than the tabloid headline version of it, you'll see that it hasn't 'gorn mad' at all and is actually fairly sensible and even mild, and is especially necessary in a kitchen where often young and/or unqualified staff daily run the gauntlet of razor-sharp knives and white-hot pans. Ignore all those stories about cheese-rolling and conkers being banned under HASAW 74: the former was prohibited by the local police because it attracted more spectators than the site could accommodate; the latter was forbidden out of fear of civil liability. In both cases HASAW was wrongly blamed as a convenient and believable scapegoat. To counter all this and ward off the chill that will strike your heart at the mere mention of the words health and safety, the Health and Safety Executive, which enforces the Act in partnership with local authority Environmental Health Officers, publishes a guide called Health and Safety Made Simple especially for small businesses: find it at **www.hse.gov.uk/simple-health-safety**.

Kitchen design and equipment

However big, however well equipped and however well designed a kitchen is, it can only cope with a finite number of diners. You are looking at moving into a shop conversion with not much more than a galley to cook in. What can you achieve?

First count your covers – that is, the number of diners you can seat. A good rule of thumb is that it takes five square feet of kitchen area to serve each diner, so if you have 60 covers you need a 28 sq m (300 sq ft) kitchen. An alternative calculation used just as commonly says that for every three square feet of dining space you need a square foot of kitchen space. The ratio differs, however, according to the standard of gastronomy you aim to provide. Fine dining takes far more space because of the number of operations being performed simultaneously and the number of staff performing them. Catering for functions, perhaps counterintuitively, takes least space because although the volume of food being cooked and plated may be greater, all the meals are exactly the same and there is only one service going on at a time. The same is true of old-fashioned grillrooms or American-style barbecue and rib shacks, and for the same reason.

Ergonomic design minimises the movement of staff as they work, which optimises the kitchen's productivity by reducing both cooking time and the number of clashes with their consequent risks of injury and spillage. Adequate ventilation and air-conditioning are also key: it's impossible to start at a brisk working pace and then accelerate as the service intensifies in an atmosphere that is steamy, possibly smoky and intolerably hot.

Choosing the equipment itself is so peculiar to each individual kitchen – its size, its dimensions and the work that it is expected to be done there – that it is impossible to do more than offer a few tips and hints. Broadly speaking, this is the minimum that a restaurant kitchen can get away with; you will probably be able to dispense with a lot if not most of it, depending on the scope of your offering.

- Stainless steel food preparation counters, one for cooked and one for raw, with conveniently located cutlery drawers and shelves and warming drawers for crockery;
- Stove(s), oven(s), grill(s), a deep-fat fryer, a microwave and specialised cookers such as a charcoal grill;
- Separate cooked and raw fridges, possibly a spare drinks fridge to restock the bar, a freezer and an ice machine;

- A dishwasher;
- A kettle-tap or old-school boiler, and tea and coffee making and serving equipment.

All of these should be of commercial standard: that is, large, robustly-built and easily accessible for cleaning and maintenance. Working surfaces should also, if possible, be of adjustable height to prevent back injuries, and step stools or kick stools should always – yes, always – be used when accessing high shelves.

A final word on equipment: if you're buying used – and the current rate of pub closures means there's a lot of it about – get it checked by an electrician before paying for it. If buying from a dealer, go for the best after-sales service and repair package you can get. It's imperative that whatever happens behind the swing doors, the show should go on – preferably without the customers (who are there to relax, after all) even realising that anything's wrong.

If brand-new equipment is too expensive, you don't have to buy second-hand: you can always lease. This ends up as more expensive in the long run, but on the other hand it reduces your borrowings and comes (or should come) with a full service and repair package. One tip, though: when leasing equipment, never accept any assurances the sales rep may make about service terms, termination conditions, etc. Reps can be very persuasive in this as in everything, but before signing any long-term agreements ALWAYS have them professionally vetted: they can be as hard to get out of as a gym membership contract!

Waste disposal

It's a perennial nuisance that short of an operating theatre a catering kitchen is meant to be about the cleanest place on earth and yet, like an operating theatre, it generates a

Utilities

A micropub and maybe even a cocktail bar need not pay much more for their utilities than a family house. But the moment you start installing chiller cabinets, ice machines, keg coolers and other commercial-grade pieces of kit then between them your kitchen, cellar and bar will expend a massive amount of electricity in heating up cold things and cooling down warm things, at great cost both to you and to the environment. It therefore makes sense to ensure all your appliances are as energy-efficient as you can make them. There are plenty of quick and easy ways that you and a competent electrician can save hundreds:

- All fixed appliances should be hardwired. Hardwiring not only reduces an appliance's electricity consumption, it also extends its life;
- If the premises is on single-phase electricity switch to three-phase;
- Change all light bulbs to low-energy or LED;
- Use a utilities broker to shop around and switch suppliers whenever advantageous.

This may be the single biggest saving you can make and, of course, it's something you can do yourself. But it's very time-consuming and demands knowledge of the market: a broker will charge a commission but will do the job far more thoroughly than you can, and you will soon notice the boost to your bottom line.

steady stream of really quite unpleasant waste. A big, busy kitchen will probably require at least two 1,100-litre wheelie bins outside the back door and a golden rule is to keep the kitchen bins empty and the wheelie bins full.

However, waste disposal is surprisingly lightly regulated. You are not legally obliged to separate your various recyclables from your landfill. Bins containing food waste must have lids with locks or latches so that rats, cats and foxes can't get at them. You mustn't overfill your wheelie bins, and you can be fined for letting overflowing waste litter the streets. And that's very nearly it. The councils and contractors who collect your rubbish are, by contrast, very heavily regulated and will sort the whole mess into bottles, cans, cardboard, paper, plastic and food waste as far as they can as they work towards their target of sending only 5 per cent of waste to landfill by 2025. Some firms will offer you a discount for separating everything yourself, and once you've got a routine going it takes very little effort to sort it as you bin it. It's an EU target, so the requirement to meet it will lapse with the UK's membership, and cuts in local authority spending mean it's unlikely to be met. However, there is still considerable consumer pressure to recycle more, and you might please a lot of customers by making a genuine and visible effort.

The exception to all this is used cooking oil, the disposal of which is regulated by your water and sewerage provider, the county council and the Environment Agency. It's terrible stuff: it collects and solidifies in drains, it's difficult for treatment plants to process and it pollutes any watercourses it reaches. And there's so much of it! Big catering kitchens and fast-food joints with deep-fat fryers tend to honour their obligation to dispose of it correctly because they use so much, but all too many smaller users, including households and some bars and smaller food businesses, whose fryers are not much bigger than domestic ones just slosh it down the sink. Well, don't!

Under the Water Act 1991 a single bar will almost certainly be too small to need a Trade Effluent Disposal Licence unless it has a microbrewery attached. But Section 111 makes you liable if you discharge anything into the sewers that causes blockage or damage, and that includes all manner of food waste, including used oil. When the Act was passed a fairly common way of disposing of old cooking oil was to use it as an ingredient in cattle-cake, but the practice was banned by the EU in 2002 and at the same time a new set of requirements was imposed. You must now keep all your used oil in a separate container; you must not let it spill; you must not pour it down a drain or sewer; and you may only allow it to be taken away by a licensed collector (your usual collector will almost certainly be licensed, but check to make sure). Most of it will be cleaned up to make biodiesel; some will be burned to generate electricity; and some will be sold to the chemical industry. All of these uses are preferable to poisoning tadpoles or giving a water vole a quiff.

Safe and legal disposal of landfill, recycling and oil does not come free, although it's not necessarily as expensive as you might think. Private companies will give you a tailor-made quote, but local councils generally publish a tariff on their websites. They range fairly widely, but you might pay your local council as little as £10 per pick-up per 1,100 litre wheelie bin of recycling or as much as £25 for 1,100 litre of landfill, so if you get a quote from a private company remember to check the local council's website too. And if it does seem a lot – well, Landfill Tax is currently nearly £90 per tonne and it only goes up.

Food without cooking

Let's start with the notion that you accept that your bottom line needs food service but that you don't want to take on

Case study
Treacle Tap, Macclesfield

The whole question of food service is something of a dilemma for the operators of small bars – not just micropubs but wine bars and cocktail lounges as well. Many don't have the space needed for storage, prepping, cooking, plating up and pot washing. Many don't have the staff. And many just don't have the inclination. If craft beer or fine wines or super-premium spirits are your absolute passion, food can be something of an afterthought.

But it needn't be and it shouldn't be. We all know that customers value a food offering of some sort, because when we offer it they buy it. And once you have dealt with the cooking and serving challenges pertinent to your own individual case, food sales can make a valuable contribution in two ways. The first is that a house speciality, or to put it bluntly a gimmick, is an attraction in itself that can generate both new and repeat custom. And secondly, snacking or grazing – the modern way of eating – adds a surprising amount of profit to a round of drinks. But the trick is not to make your food offering, however minimal, an afterthought. In such a tiny arena as yours every part of the offering has to shine. So polish it up and show it off and less really can be more.

A very good example of this approach is the Treacle Tap in Macclesfield, Cheshire, somewhat mysteriously known as 'Treacletown'. Converted from an old saddlery in 2010 by Bronwyn Riley and her nephew Jordan, the micropub will accommodate 60 customers if none of them want to breathe and it only runs to three hand-pumps, which makes for limited choice but a terrific turnover and hence ideal quality. The real ales are supplemented by three keg taps sporting exotic foreign elixirs and a big range of bottled beers from all over the world. As is usual in similar set-ups the range of food is limited, but it's more mixed than some. Listed on a very well-presented menu rather than just scrawled on a board, the cold snacks include not only those sturdy micropub staples ham, cheese and pork pie, but also a selection of yer foreign muck – olives, hummus and continental meats. There's a range of locally made cakes and traybakes as well for those with a sweet tooth. At very modest prices ranging from £1.50 to £3.90 and served until 10.00 pm, these are impulse buys – snacks and nibbles that customers might treat themselves to on a whim as many times in an evening as they fancy.

The star attraction, though, is the range of locally made pies, with vegetarian as well as meat fillings, served hot with mash, peas (garden or mushy) and gravy. At £8.90 (or £7.90 with salad and chutney instead of mash, peas and gravy) they're a substantial meal, and their importance is revealed by the fact that they're cited as often and as prominently as the beer in the Treacle Tap's many online rave reviews.

Bronwyn's husband, Tim Sedgwick, gave up his day job to join the firm in 2012 and has helped steer it through expansion to a chain of three (so far), the others being the Young Pretender in Congleton and the Old Dancer (formerly a lap-dancing club) in Wilmslow. They're both rather bigger than the Treacle Tap and their menus are bigger too: similar in inspiration – a mixture of impulse-priced nibbles and more substantial meals – but with paninis, sandwiches, sharing plates and soup.

Food service, says Tim, was never an afterthought. "It was always part of Bronwyn's vision, and we have always understood the importance of it," he says. "It may not be a huge percentage of your total sales, but if you have four people sitting down to a drink and they each have a couple of pints and something to eat as well – well, that's quite a big transaction. But you do need to be thoughtful about what you do. When you have a small but highly concentrated menu then everything on it has to be absolutely top quality."

what is, in effect, a parallel business and are deterred by all the food-related bureaucracy described above. Don't be downhearted: there are options.

The simplest is to allow your customers to order takeaways and provide them with crockery and cutlery, maybe at a nominal charge to cover the cost of dishwashing and breakages. You don't make a penny profit out of this (unless you charge the local takeaways a sly commission), but you do keep your customers satisfied, create a more convivial atmosphere and boost your wet sales.

Next up in the order of complexity is to invest in a fridge and lay in a stock of ready-made sandwiches and other cold snacks. You have to register with environmental health and you will have your inspection, but unless you're egregiously slatternly it should really only be a formality. You can get quite adventurous with this, too: wholesalers today will supply a very wide range of sandwiches, pies, pasties, wraps, meze, paninis, fajitas, bruschettas, tapas, canapés, sushi and other ready-made deli delights absolutely perfect for quick-serve lunches, for the early evening crowd who've dropped in after work and haven't had their tea yet, for the late-evening crowd who've had a couple of pints and now have the munchies and for customers in general whose peckishness isn't quite satisfied by a bag of Wotsits. The same wholesalers will also supply pots or sachets of sauces and chutneys, so you don't even have to go to the trouble of opening a jar. Do, however, taste every ready-made item you plan to serve. Some are better than others, and although you yourself may have done no more than warm up a pitta, decant some dips into nice white ramekins and then arrange them all artfully on a big white plate, every failure is your failure just as surely as every triumph is your triumph.

These are the simpler options that will enable you to run a convincing food operation on a shoestring. Cooking from fresh is a very different matter. A few Full English fry-ups in the morning shouldn't prove too much of a challenge, and you can always make up individual portions of standard dishes – preferably gratins such as macaroni cheese, cottage pie, cannelloni, lasagne and moussaka because they don't dry out too quickly – in the morning for microwaving to order. Anything much more complicated or on a larger scale takes us into restaurant territory and rather beyond the scope of this book.

09

Appendices

Appendix I 200
Appendix II 207
Directory of services and suppliers 210
Index 222

Appendix I
Negotiating a lease

The thrust of this book has been to persuade aspiring licensees to strike out on their own rather than seek the (illusory?) shelter of a corporate lease. Circumstance or preference might drive you to the latter course, though, and provided your eyes and ears are wide open, you accept nothing at face value and take exhaustive professional advice (no, not just seek – take!) you may very well strike a genuinely equitable deal with no obstacles to your success. A few negotiating tips can't harm, though.

Buying an existing lease

In the normal course of events you would be buying the remaining years of an unexpired lease from an existing lessee. In this situation the lessee has no power to vary the terms and conditions he or she originally wrung from the lessor, however many years ago. Still, if you can't get the terms you want, you always have the option of walking away, and if you or your professional advisers are in the slightest doubt that's exactly what you should do.

One thing that should set off an alarm in lease negotiations is any reluctance on the vendor's part to open up the books. Buying a portion of a lease is not like taking a tenancy: in this case you're buying a business and you have a right to see the books. At very least you should have full access to VAT returns going back two years, and if they're not forthcoming don't waste any more of your time. But the books should also provide other information about the state of repair of the building, fixed overheads such as business rates and mandatory insurances and – it's vital to know this – the seasonality of the trade. Some pubs do two-thirds of their business between April and September and are hardly worth opening in January and February (except for Burns Night and Valentine's Day, of course). Without this kind of detail you can't work out what staffing levels you'll need and when, and you can't make a cash-flow projection for your business plan... and without a business plan you won't be able to raise the finance you need. (Your mortgage lender will also most probably want a structural survey too, and as the lease will be full-repairing the survey might have a decisive bearing on whether you want to proceed.) Having said that, the accounts will only show how the pub traded under the outgoing lessee, who will have built up personal goodwill that will be lost when the lease is transferred. It is important to always bear in mind, therefore, that past performance is no guarantee of future profit.

Negotiating a new lease

Sometimes the pub that takes your fancy will be vacant and you will have to negotiate an entirely new lease. The first thing you and your advisers will want to know, of course, is why it is vacant. Your first suspicion will be that the pub company imposed such onerous conditions that when a downturn in trade came along the business proved unsustainable. That may very well be the case, although it's possible that the previous lessee was at fault in some way; but from your point of view it's safest to assume that the lessor rode the business too hard. In this case you are not actually entitled to see the pub's books, but if at all possible contact the previous lessee and suppliers who will readily tell you how successful the business was in reality. And make sure you get a written statement of the pub's historic barrelage from the lessor. Even if, as we said above, past performance is no guarantee of future profit, to proceed without a fairly strong idea of the pub's trading history can and often does prove ruinous.

Don't take the lessor's unsupported word for the pub's potential. Pub companies and their brokers will naturally seek to persuade you that the establishment has been underperforming for this reason or that, and with a bit of work and investment it could trade at a much higher level. But optimistic estimates of potential barrelage, however enthusiastic and sincere they seem, are very often no more than a trap for the unwary, and every prospective lessee should remember the context, which is that since 2007 the nation's pubs have seen a drop of around 25 per cent in barrelage.

Valuation
Armed with all this information you have a working idea of what your target pub's Fair Maintainable Trade (FMT) is – that is, what it has done in the past and ought to do in the future. You use this to calculate its open market rental value, which should represent what would be paid by a Reasonably Efficient Operator (who is assumed to have reasonable knowledge and skill and to have taken professional advice) based on FMT.

Start by estimating how much of that FMT is likely to be gross profit. For this you really will need a stocktaker with local experience, who will be able to advise fairly swiftly on the likely gross profit achievable at given prices and will have a history of knowledge and databases of examples. Tied operators' typical wet GPs have remained fairly stable over the years at around 50 per cent, but it can be significantly lower where there is free-of-tie or managed house competition or where customers are particularly sensitive to price increases. In a district where these conditions prevail, you have two choices: you grit your teeth and accept that you will have to work on the basis of a lower GP or you can seek to share the pain with the lessor by negotiating discounts. And to be fair, many agreements already contain provision for tied product price discounts.

Operating costs aside from rent – utilities including waste collection; business rates; insurance premiums and other professional fees and service charges; repairs, maintenance and depreciation; and above all staff costs – are then subtracted from the GP. The British Beer & Pub Association produces an excellent guide, sensibly called *Running a Pub*, which is available on the BBPA's own and many member brewery's websites, but any sensible prospective operator would also turn to an accountant for help in putting together a business plan. Indeed, many pub companies and brewers protect themselves by requiring proof that the operator has taken professional advice before signing the agreement. With the benefit of an accountant's knowledge and experience in trade-related properties, a good estimate of the likely operating costs should be established. Previous accounts and industry benchmarking information will help in the estimation of likely costs. According to Association of Licensed Multiple Retailers, benchmarking taken across multiple and single operators, average overheads amount to around 40 per cent of GP. They would be higher in pubs with substantial food sales and accommodation, and lower in smaller wet-led operations.

The result of this subtraction is the net profit before rent, also called the 'divisible balance' because it is the amount to be shared between lessor and lessee. A rule of thumb often used, but by no means mandatory, is a 50:50 split. In certain circumstances this split will vary. If the divisible balance is below about £60,000 then it could be argued that the lessee should take a higher proportion of it, and there is case law (Brooker v Unique) to support this idea.

It's worth bearing in mind how serious an impact getting either GP or overheads even slightly wrong can have. Overestimating these even a little can reduce the lessee's earnings substantially without reducing the lessor's share of the split at all. The list of variables that can cause such a tiny miscalculation is almost endless and, in many cases, highly technical. So always seek genuinely independent advice and be wary of accountants, surveyors and indeed solicitors who regularly act for pub companies. Always ask your prospective professional advisors, however rude the question seems, who their best customers are so that you can take a measured view of the advice they offer. It's your future that's at stake, after all!

Having agreed a rent, there's one more thing to remember: at subsequent rent reviews the lessee should not be penalised for improving trade through goodwill they have created or improvements they have made. Equally, the company should not suffer if the lessee trades less well than should be expected of an REO.

Small Business Act 2015

Leasehold rents are generally reviewed every three or five years and some also increase annually in line with inflation. But over the 30 years since long leases were invented it has always seemed to lessees that rents were only reviewed upwards. When factories closed, when unemployment soared and when disposable incomes plunged, rents only ever went up – as did wholesale prices for tied products. The pub companies, which were built on a foundation of debt, couldn't afford to lighten up: rents and MPOs were chased remorselessly, and if anyone defaulted – well, there were plenty more where they came from. The final slap in the face for many harassed lessees was the enforced installation of flow-monitoring equipment in their cellars. It was as if the pub companies didn't believe that they were genuinely selling so little beer and had concluded that they must be buying outside the tie.

That, at least, is how many lessees whose businesses were failing saw it – and indeed many still do. Of course there are plenty of lessees whose businesses aren't failing but flourishing, but particularly in the earliest days of the long lease any positive stories seemed hard to believe. Not only was the recession of 1990–93 the longest since the Great Depression, with very high unemployment hitting the licensed trade particularly hard, but the tenanted trade's long-standing representative bodies, local Licensed Victuallers' Associations, were in meltdown: their umbrella organisation, the National LVA, actually folded in 1992 (although successor bodies such as the Federation of Licensed Victuallers Associations (FLVA) and the PAS have filled many of the gaps left by its demise). Isolated, disorganised and vulnerable in the face of their landlords' intransigence, angry lessees fought a long-running guerrilla war during which ad hoc organisations were formed and dissolved, legal challenges – one of them going all the way to the European Court of Justice before failing – were mounted, petitions were raised and MPs were lobbied. Even Prince Charles pitched in as patron of the Pub is the Hub promotional campaign.

Over many years these efforts became more coherent, more organised and more sophisticated, and in time they paid off when the campaigners succeeded in having not just a few clauses but an entirely new section – almost a bill in itself – inserted into the Small

Businesses Bill that became Part 4 of the Small Businesses Act 2015. This was a triumph of lobbying by licensed trade representatives and in theory it gives lessees and tenants of the bigger pub companies a greater degree of power and influence over their own destinies than they have ever had before.

The Code, which came into force in July 2016, is binding on all companies, brewing or non-brewing, that own 500 or more pubs. It is overseen by an adjudicator to whom lessees can refer their grievances and who has the power to investigate to make a resolution, and to enforce his judgments with financial penalties in certain circumstances. In many respects the Code confines itself to giving legal force to the best practices that have emerged since 1988, and a great deal of it is taken up with rent assessments and arbitration, as you might expect. But one provision in particular is really quite radical and poses an interesting challenge for both lessor and lessee, and that provision is the Market Rent Only option or MRO.

The practice of rentalising all or part of the tie has been around for many years, although it hasn't been exactly commonplace. MRO gives lessees the opportunity to put their money where their mouths have always been and to find out for themselves whether paying an independently assessed market rent and being free to buy from whatever suppliers they like will really make them better off. There are some who suspect that their rent would actually go down when independently assessed, even when they pay to opt out of the tie. Having said that, MRO was a resounding failure to start with. In its first year of operation 497 lessees applied but only 11 succeeded in negotiating an MRO lease, and the adjudicator had to order an inquiry into the pub companies' obstructive tactics to try and get the whole mess back on course. On the face of it – and these are early days – the code of practice looks like a rerun of Children's Certificates: well-meaning but vastly over elaborate, missing the central point and easy to frustrate.

A very detailed discussion of the minutiae of MRO has been jointly put together by the BII, the FLVA and the Association of Licensed Multiple Retailers in Q&A format and can be found on their websites.

A non-binding voluntary version of the code exists for companies that own fewer than 500 pubs, but since 2010 they have had their own voluntary arbitration mechanism that seems to have gained wide acceptance. An umbrella group called the Pubs Governing Body and comprising the BBPA, the BII, the ALMR, the FLVA, the Guild of Master Victuallers and the Brighton & Hove Licensees' Association runs two schemes – the Pubs Independent Rent Review Scheme and the Pubs Independent Conciliation & Arbitration Service – on behalf of 37 smaller pub chains, most of which are brewers. As the voluntary code for these below-500 companies doesn't include the MRO option it's hard to see much of an incentive for it to replace the PGB mechanisms.

Appendix II
Staffing miscellany

The realm of human resources and employment law is vast, expansive, riven with impassable crevasses, bereft of roads and inhabited by trolls, ogres and vengeful wraiths. Fortunately it's mostly beyond the scope of this book – we are giving both the swamp of grievance procedure and the desert of equal opportunities a very wide berth within these pages – but you have to know it all and must seek out the wisdom of specialists or risk the consequences: www.gov.uk/browse/employing-people would be a good place to start. In the meantime, here are three employment issues you will definitely run up against.

Pension plans

It used to be that starting a pension plan at work was something of a rite of passage: a step in the transition from youth and apprenticeship to adulthood and permanence. And when employment-related pensions were more or less voluntary, especially in the hospitality sector, starting a plan created something of an unspoken bond between employer and employee – a sign of mutual confidence and an intention to make a long-term commitment to each another.

Now that workplace pensions for over-22s earning £10,000 a year or more are compulsory, that significance has disappeared. But there is still a simple way employers can use workplace pensions to attract and retain staff: pay into them. The law only requires employees to pay in – up to 3 per cent of their income above £5,876 – but it is perfectly possible for you to create an incentive by adding a (tax-deductible) sum of your own. Pensions are always a political football, though, constantly subject to alteration and reform: refer to **www.gov.uk/workplace-pensions-employers** but always consult your accountant as well for up-to-the-minute information.

Tips and tax

Tips are an essential part of your staff's income; indeed for top mixologists tips and gratuities make up more than half of it. So how well they do out of tips is going to play an important part in both recruitment and retention.

You are legally obliged to pay all staff at least the National Living Wage – £7.83 an hour as of April 2018 – and tips are strictly extra. All tips are liable for income tax, but there are ways you can avoid Employer's National Insurance Contributions (legally!), depending on how the tips are paid to the staff. Broadly speaking, there are three methods:

- Cash paid directly by customers to the member of staff who served them. This is a less and less common way of paying in the era of plastic, but any cash that changes hands is the member of staff's property and that member of staff is responsible for declaring it to HMRC. Alternatively, the member of staff may pool it as part of the tronc (defined as 'a common fund into which tips and service charges are paid for distribution to staff', see below).
- Service charge/card gratuity paid to you. You can pay each member of staff their card gratuity and the portion of the service charge to which they are entitled as part of their monthly pay packet, in which case you will have to deduct and pay the income tax due and Employer's NI contribution in the normal way. You are allowed to make deductions from the service charge to cover bank charges, administration fees, breakages, stock shortages and so on – in fact you don't have to share the service charge with your staff at all – but these deductions must be set out clearly in their contracts of employment.
- Tronc. Service charges, card gratuities and possibly cash tips are handed to the designated troncmaster (who may not be the employer or manager) to be distributed among all staff according to an agreed ratio. This is a way of making sure that the front of house staff don't get to hog all the tips! The troncmas-

ter must register the tronc with HMRC, and you are obliged to make sure that this is done. After that, though, your involvement is over: no admin and no NI contributions, although you may volunteer to help the troncmaster by processing the income tax payments due through your PAYE without incurring liability for NICs.

It can't be stressed enough that it's in your best interests to keep deductions to a minimum – and it's preferable not to make any deductions at all – and to ensure that tips are divided fairly between the waiters and the mixologists etc., or you won't be able to attract or keep decent staff in the future. And as you depend on your staff's ability and attitude to build the repeat custom you're going to need, you'd be foolish to risk running an unhappy ship by rooking your workers out of what will only come to a measly sum in the end.

Taxis home for late workers

It has long been customary for bar and restaurant proprietors to pay for taxis home for late-night staff, especially female staff. However, HMRC makes it perfectly plain that it regards the cost of travel to and from work as the employee's responsibility and, except in certain circumstances, extra pay made to cover it is taxable.

Disability is one of the special circumstances, but time of travel, by and large, isn't. The only circumstances under which employers can pay taxi fares tax-free (and ENICs-free) are:
- If it's an irregular occurrence, not a result of ordinary working hours.
- If it's too late for public transport.
- If it would be unreasonable to expect the employee to use public transport.

Only the first 60 journeys a year are tax-exempt, and the employer must keep detailed records of each occasion when they pay for a taxi. Section 248 of the Employers' Income Manual, updated 2017, gives the topic three whole pages. It should be noted that taxi fares for early travel – for waiting staff coming in for breakfast service, for example – are never exempt.

Directory of Services and Suppliers

Note: A complete listing of drinks producers is simply not possible. There are perhaps 2,000 brewers, 450 winemakers, 300 or more distillers and an unknown and unknowable number of independent cidermakers in the UK, as well as hundreds of shippers and distributors of imports. The nearest thing there is to a complete and up-to-date directory of cask ale brewers published annually is found in CAMRA's Good Beer Guide.

General drinks wholesalers

434 Enterprises
Kingston Bagpuize, Oxford OX13 5AS
Tel +44 (0) 1865 823333
www.434enterprises.co.uk
Contact: Martin Allen

ABV Wholesale
Pitt St, Keighley BD21 4PE
Tel +44 (0) 1535 669966
www.abvwholesale.com
Contact: Ross Sleightholme

AF Blakemore
Rose Hill, Willenhall, WV13 2JP
Tel +44 (0) 1902 366066
Contact: Russell Grant

Ale & Beer Supplies
East Side Ind. Est, St Helens, WA9 3AS
Tel +44 (0) 1744 22023

www.aleandbeers.co.uk
Contact: Christopher Lawler

ASD
Brookside Way, Huthwaite, NG17 2N
Tel +44 (0) 1623 441427
www.asdwholesale.co.uk
Contact: Steven Seaman

Battlefield Beers
Archers Way, Shrewsbury, SY1 3AB
Tel +44 (0) 1743 467163
www.battlefieldbeers.co.uk
Contact: John Pitcher.

Beer Trading Co.
Nantwich Rd, Middlewich, CW10 0LH
Tel +44 (0) 1606 841467
www.beertrading.co.uk

Casa Julia
11 Springwood Drive,

Braintree, CM7 2YN
Tel +44 (0) 1376 320269
www.casajulia.co.uk
Contact: Vincenzo Santomauro

Morecambe Bay Wines
Whitelund Ind. Est, Morecambe
LA3 3PT
Tel +44 (0) 1524 39481
www.baywines.co.uk
Contacts: Peter Cross, Malcolm Savage

Morgenrot Group
Unit 2, Canary Way, Swinton
M27 8AW
Tel +44 (0) 845 070 4310
www.morgenrot.co.uk
Contact: John Critchley

Nectar Imports
Berwick St Leonards, Wilts,
SP3 5GN
Tel +44 (0) 1747 840100
www.nectar.net
Contacts: Simon Dodd, Mark or Fiona Jukes

Cascade Drinks
Bowerhill, Melksham SN12 6TJ Tel +44 (0) 1225 708842
www.molesbrewery.com
Contact: Roger Catte

Colemans ABC
The Old Tram Depot,
St Leonards, TN38 8BG
Tel +44 (0) 1424 71777
www.colemansabc.co.uk
Contact: David Coleman

Dayla Ltd
50 Aylesbury Rd, Aston Clinton,
HP22 5AH
Tel +44 (0) 1296 630013
www.dayladrinks.co.uk
Contact: Tim Cooper

DeeBee Wholesale
Adam Smith St, Grimsby
DN31 1SJ
Tel +44 (0) 1472 313200
www.deebee.co.uk
Contact: Paddy O'Connor

Edwards Beers & Minerals
5 Grovebury Place, Grovebury Rd,
Leighton Buzzard LU7 4SH Tel +44 (0) 1525 372290
www.edwardsdrinks.com
Contact: Terry Edwards

Free Trade Beers & Minerals
Gascoigne Rd, Barking IG11 7LN
Tel +44 (0) 0208 477 4650
www.freetradebeers.co.uk
Contacts: Ranveer Singh Mohal, Satwant Singh

Halls Drinks
Greenfield Business Park,
Holywell CH8 7HJ
Tel +44 (0) 1352 711444
www.hallsdrinks.co.uk

Heathwick
25A Holland St W8 4NA
Tel +44 (0) 207 938 3991
www.heathwick.com
Contacts: Marc Krens, John Rodenhouse

Hills Prospect
Consolidated House, Faringdon Ave, Harold Hill RM3 8SP
Tel +44 (0) 1708 33 050
www.hillsprospect.com
Contact: Trevor Bowers

HT Drinks
31 Park Royal Rd, London, NW10 7LQ
Tel +44 (0) 208 963 3130
www.htdrinks.co.uk
Contacts: Prakash or Sanjay Thakrar

Imbibe Drinks
The IO Centre, River Rd, Barking IG11 0DR
Tel +44 (0) 208 591 9001
www.imbibe-drinks.com
Contact: Steve Moody

IM Wines
Vulcan Way, New Addington, London, CR0 9UG
Tel +44 (0) 1689 841800
www.imwines.co.uk
Contact: David Russell

Inn Express
Haselor, Alcester B49 6LX
Tel +44 (0) 1789 488008
www.inn-express.com
Contact: Richard Hall

Island Ales
Yarmouth Rd, Shalfleet, Isle of Wight, PO30 4LZ
Tel +44 (0) 1938 821731
www.islandales.co.uk
Contact: Steve Minshull

J&A Drinks
Throop Rd
Bournemouth BH8 0DL
Tel +44 (0) 1202 539494
www.jandadrinks.co.uk
Contacts: Jonathon Horton (Snr & Jnr); Maggie Horton; Anthony Horton

Joseph Keegan & Sons
Cleveland Ave, Holyhead LL65 2LB
Tel +44 (0) 1407 762333
www.josephkeegan.co.uk
Contact: Francis Campbell MD

Libra Drinks
Lenton Lane Ind. Est, Nottingham NG7 2NN
Tel +44 (0) 845 130 1623
www.libradrinks.com
Contact: Gary Beagley MD

LWC
Stainburn Rd, Openshaw, M11 2DN
Tel +44 (0) 161 438 4060
www.lwc-drinks.co.uk
Contact: Ebrahim Mukadam

Maison Maurice
North Fleet Ind. Est, North Fleet DA11 9BL
Tel +44 (0) 1474 361200
www.maisonmaurice.co.uk
Contacts: Adrian or Jonathan Sundin

Matthew Clark
Whitchurch Lane, Bristol, BS14 0JZ

Directory of Services and Suppliers

Tel +44 (0) 1275 891400
www.matthewclark.co.uk

Middleton Wholesale
Weedon Rd Ind. Est,
Northampton NN5 5AF
Tel +44 (0) 1604 750040
www.middletonwholesale.com
Contact: Nick Middleton.

Ooberstock
9 Queen's Square, Ascot
Business Park, Ascot SL5 9FE
Tel +44 (0) 844 493 0000
www.ooberstock.com
Contact: Stephen Brogan

One Way Wholesale
Anglian Ind. Est, Atcost Rd, Barking IG11 0EG
Tel +44 (0) 208 500 1600
www.onewaywholesale.co.uk
Contacts: Kuldeep Bihal, Kulvarn Gill

Page & Sons
Hopes Lane, Ramsgate
CT12 6UW
Tel +44 (0) 1843 591214
www.pageandsons.co.uk
Contact: Jonathan Hatch Page

Primo Drinks
Bredbury Park Ind. Est,
Stockport SK6 2ST
Tel +44 (0) 161 406 0606
www.primodrinks.co.uk
Contact: Brian Wright

Spencers (Bromsgrove) Ltd
Sanders Road, Bromsgrove
B61 7AR
Tel +44 (0) 1527 831070
www.bromsgrove-ltd.co.uk
Contact: Stephen Thompson

Swallow Drinks
Stonehouse Lane, Birmingham
B32 3AH
Tel +44 (0) 121 428 6850
www.swallow.uk.com
Contact: Stephen Land (Sr)

Temple Wines
Church Lane NW9 8UA
Tel +44 (0) 208 905 9484
www.templewines.co.uk
Contact: Rajni or Nalin Kataria

Tolchards
Silverhills Rd, Newton Abbot
TQ12 5ND
Tel +44 (0) 1626 333426
www.tolchards.com
Contacts: James, Sean or Steven Mardell

TotalServe Wholesale
Arbour Lane, Knowsley L33 7XE
Tel +44 (0) 151 549 0151
www.jeroboam-and-schott.co.uk
Contacts: Thomas Clarke,
Jonathon Finn

Turner & Wrights
Vine House Way, Lostock, Bolton
BL6 4TW
Tel +44 (0) 1204 673010
www.turnerandwrights.co.uk
Contact: Martin Gilmore

VC Vintners
Marine Park, Gapton Hall Road,
Great Yarmouth NR31 0NL
Tel +44 (0) 1493 667586
www.vcvintners.co.uk

Venus plc
Garman Rd London N17 0UT
Tel +44 (0) 1208 801 0011
www.venusplc.com
Contact: Kerry Michael

Wigan Beer Co
Victoria Trading Est, Miry Lane,
Wigan WN3 4BW
Tel +44 (0) 1942 821711
www.wiganbeer.co.uk
Contact: Adam Jones

WJ Armstrong
12 London Rd, East Grinstead
RH19 1AG
Tel +44 (0) 1342 215752
www.wjarmstrong.com

Wild's of Oldham
Westwood Ind. Est, Arkwright St,
Oldham OL9 9LZ
Tel +44 (0) 161 626 1990
www.wildsofoldham.co.uk
Contacts: Steven or Andrew Wild

Young's Beers
Wines & Spirits, Lomeshaye Ind.
Est, Nelson BB9 6RT
Tel +44 (0) 1282 617775
www.youngsbeerswinesspirit-sltd.co.uk
Contacts: John Stephenson or
Albert Young.

Beer and cider specialist wholesalers

AVS Wines & Beers
Canal Rd, Gravesend DA12 2PA
Tel +44 (0) 1474 537767
www.avscaskbeers.co.uk
Contacts: Linda Rush or Ray Roussell

Beer Direct
10 Ferndale Close, Werrington,
Stoke ST9 0PW
Tel +44 (0) 1782 303823
www.beer-direct.co.uk
Contacts: Martin or Phil Johnson

Beer Gonzo
3A Earlsdon St, Coventry
CV5 6EP
Tel +44 (0) 247 667 1980
www.beergonzo.co.uk
Beer Paradise
Unit 20, Marston Moor Business
Park, Tockwith YO26 7QF
Tel +44 (0) 1423 359533
www.beerparadise.co.uk
Contact: Zak Avery

Beer Hawk
Ash Way, Thorp Arch Ind. Est,
Wetherby LS23 7FU
Tel +44 (0) 1423 525750
www.beerhawk.co.uk
Contact: Russ Clarke

Biercraft
53 Coopersdale Rd E9 6AU
Tel +44 (0) 7818 685060
www.biercraft.co.uk
Contact: Nick Trower

Directory of Services and Suppliers

Brewers Wholesale
Rufford Rd, Stourbridge DY9 7ND
Tel +44 (0) 1384 374050
www.thebrewerswholesale.co.uk
Contact: Mark Hill

Cave Direct
Unit B10, Larkfield Trad. Est, New Hythe Lane, Larkfield ME20 6SW
Tel +44 (0) 1622 710339
www.cavedirect.com
Contact: Bart Verhaeghe

James Clay
River Street, Brighouse HD6 1LU
Tel +44 (0) 1422 377560
www.jamesclay.co.uk
Contact: Ian Clay

C.O.D. Beers
3 Moulsecoomb Way, Brighton BN2 4PB
Tel +44 (0) 1273 626604
www.cod-beers.co.uk
Contact: Peter Bell

Euroboozer
Notley Farm, Abbots Langley WD5 0GX
Tel +44 (0) 1923 263335
www.euroboozer.co.uk
Contact: Martyn Railton

Flying Firkin
Holker Mill, Burnley Rd, Colne BB8 8JN
Tel +44 (0) 1282 865923
www.flyingfirkin.co.uk
Contact: Nina Bates

German Beer Co.
33 Great Guildford St, London SE1 0FA
Tel +44 (0) 207 159 3539
www.buygermanbeer.co.uk
Contact: Timo Breunig

Jolly Good Beer
Riverdale Organic Farm, Upwell, Wisbech PE14 9A
Tel +44 (0) 800 043 2337
www.jollygoodbeer.co.uk
Contact: Yvan Seth

Pierhead
The Paddocks, Wood Street, Swanley Village, Kent BR8 7PA Tel +44 (0) 1322 662377
www.pierhead.uk.com
Contacts: Amanda Nokes, Sam Calver, Ian Hercules

Pig's Ears Beer Trade
Ridge Farm, Rowhook, Surrey RH12 3QB
Tel +44 (0) 1306 627779
www.pigs-ears.co.uk
Contact: Toni Skinner

Real Ale Ltd
Richmond Rd, Twickenham TW1 2EF
Tel +44 (0) 208 892 3710
www.realale.com
Contact: Richard Sharp

Real Beer Company
Dragoon Close, Heathfield Ind. Est, Newton Abbot TQ12 6TU
Tel +44 (0) 845 241 1122

www.therealbeercompany.co.uk
Contact: Martin Breading

Small Beer
Churchill Business Park,
Bracebridge Heath, Lincoln
LN4 2FF
Tel +44 (0) 1522 540431
www.smallbeerwholesale.co.uk
Contact: Rob Eastwood

Vertical Drinks
Kirkstall Brewery, 100 Kirkstall
Road, Leeds LS3 1HJ
Tel +44 (0) 113 898 0280
www.vwrticaldrinks.com
Contact: Steve Holt

Westside Drinks
126 Newgate St, London
EC1A 7AA
Tel +44 (0) 208 996 2000
www.westsidedrinks.co.uk
Contact: George McNicol

World Beers
Allen House, Station Rd,
Sawbridgeworth, Herts
CM21 9JX
Tel +44 (0) 1279 600044
www.world-beers.co.uk
Contact: Peter Karsten

Wines and spirits

Amathus Drinks
309 Elvedon Rd, London,
NW10 7ST
Tel +44 (0) 208 951 9840
www.amathusdrinks.com
Contacts: Harry Georgiou (CEO),
Fraser McGuire / Simon Bradbury

Bacchus Wine
38 Market Pl., Olney MK46 4AJ Tel
+44 (0) 1234 711140
www.bacchus.co.uk
Contacts: Russell & Antoinette
Heap

Bibendum
113 Regents Park Rd, London
NW1 8UR
Tel +44 (0) 207 449 4120
www.bibendum-wine.co.uk

Champers Wholesale
263 Water Rd, Wembley London
HA0 1HX
Tel +44 (0) 208 961 2889
www.champerswholesale.com

Derventio Wines
Castlegate, Malton YO17 7EE
Tel +44 (0) 1653 693193
www.derventiowines.co.uk
Contact: Paul Tate-Smith

Enotria & Coe
23 Cumberland Avenue, London
NW10 7RX
Tel +44 (0) 208 961 4411
www.enotriacoe.com
Contact: Matt Davies

Hallgarten Wines
Dallow Rd, Luton LU1 1UR
Tel +44 (0) 1582 722538
www.hdnwines.co.uk

Impact Brands
Clarke Ind. Est, St Mowden Rd,

Stretford M32 0ZF
Tel +44 (0) 333 344 8500 / 07718 964370
www.impactbrands.co.uk
Contact: Peter Rossiter

The Grapevine Wine Service
Threlkeld CA12 4SU
Tel +44 (0) 17687 76100
www.grapevinewineservices.co.uk
Contacts: Ben Paxon / Chris Holland / Shelley Daly

Tanner's Wines
26 Wyle Cop, Shrewsbury SY1 1XD.
Tel +44 (0) 1743 234500
www.tanners-wines.co.uk
Contacts: James Tanner or Stephen Lloyd

Telford Wines
Ercall House, Stafford Park, Telford TF3 3BD
Tel +44 (0) 1952 291129
www.telfordwines.co.uk
Contact: Nick Gent

Wines of Interest
Burlington Rd, Ipswich IP1 2HS
Tel +44 (0) 1473 215752
www.winesofinterest.co.uk
Contact: Jonathan Hare

Treasury Wine Estates
Regal House, London Rd, Twickenham TW1 3QS
Tel +44 (0) 208 843 8400
www.tweglobal.com

Bar and cellar equipment and services

A-Cask
St Andrews Ind. Est, Bridport, DT6 3EX
Tel +44 (0) 1308 426982
www.acask.com
Contacts: Philip Smith or Russell Warren

BOC Sureserve
Priestley Rd, Worsley M28 2UT
Tel +44 (0) 800 111333
www.boconline.co.uk

Brewfitt
Penistone Rd, Huddersfield HD8 0LE
Tel +44 (0) 1484 340800
www.brewfitt.com
Contacts: Curtis or James Paxman

Epos Group
Newington Rd, Ramsgate CT12 6EE
Tel +44 (0) 870 428 2830
www.eposgroup.co.uk

GS Systems
Buxton Rd, Stockport SK2 6LR
Tel +44 (0) 800 655 6246
www.gs-systems.co.uk

Orderella
Marble Arch Tower, 55 Bryanston St, London, W1H 7AA
Tel +44 (0) 203 617 0540
www.orderella.co.uk

Williams Refrigeration
Bryggen Rd, North Lynn Ind.
Est, King's Lynn PE30 2HZ
Tel +44 (0) 1553 817000
www.williams-refrigeration.co.uk

Zenith Hygiene
Dixons Hill Rd, Welwyn Green,
Herts AL9 7JE
Tel +44 (0) 1707 270260
www.zhgplc.com

Catering supplies, equipment and sundries

Bidvest Foodservice
Thomas Rd, Wooburn Green,
HP10 0PE
Tel +44 (0) 1494 555900
www.bidvest.co.uk
Contact: Andrew Selley CEO

Booker Wholesale
Equity House, Irthlingborough
Rd, Wellingborough NN8 1LT
Tel +44 (0) 1933 371000
www.booker.co.uk

Global Foods
Stadium Close, Cardiff CF11 8TS
Tel +44 (0) 7747 633306
www.globalfoods.co.uk
Contacts: Mubarik Ali,
Mohammed Yakub

Petty Wood Ltd
Livingstone Rd, Andover,
SP10 5NS
Tel +44 (0) 1264 345 500
www.pettywood.co.uk

Pub Food Direct
Enfield Ind. Est, Redditch,
B97 6BG
Tel +44 (0) 1527 593907
www.pubfooddirect.co.uk

Reynolds, Brittania Rd
Waltham Cross EN8 7RQ
Tel +44 (0) 845 310 6200
www.reynolds-cs.com
Steelite International
Orme St, Stoke-on-Trent ST6 3RB
Tel +44 (0) 1782 829000
www.steelite.com

Professional services

Control Energy Costs
Tollers Farm, Drive Rd,
Coulsdon CR5 1BN
Tel +44 (0) 1737 556631
www.cec.uk.com
Contact: Phil Ager

David Jones Accountants
Tel +44 (0) 1937 583356
www.drjaccountants.co.uk

Joelson Wilson & Co. solicitors
30 Portland Place, London, W1B 1LZ
Tel +44 (0) 207 580 5721
www.joelsonwilson.com

John Gaunt & Partners, solicitors
Tel +44 (0) 114 266 8664
www.john-gaunt.co.uk

Kuit Steinart Levy solicitors
St Mary's Passage, Manchester,

Directory of Services and Suppliers

M3 2RD
Tel +44 (0) 161 838 7888
www.kuits.com

Lunn Groves solicitors
158 Hagley Rd, Old Swinford,
DY8 2JL
Tel +44 (0) 1384 397 355
www.lunngroves.co.uk

Polaris Business Systems
Hi-Point House, Thomas St,
Taunton TA2 6HB
Tel +44 (0) 1823 335 292
www.fbh.co.uk

Poppleston Allen solicitors
37 Stoney St, The Lace Market,
Nottingham NG1 1LS
Tel +44 (0) 1159 538 500
www.popall.co.uk

Praxis42 Health & Safety
Training / Consultancy
Crockatt Rd, Hadleigh, IP7 6RJ Tel +44 (0) 870 466 4201
www.praxis42.com

Sentient solicitors/general consultants
49 Pegholme, Ilkley Road, Otley LS21 3JP Tel +44 (0) 3456 446006
www.sentientuk.co.uk

Screach Media & Marketing
The Kiln, Hoults Yard, Walker Rd,
Newcastle upon Tyne,
NE6 2HL
Tel +44 (0) 345 113 3888
www.screach.com

**Shield Consultancy Services
health & safety/hygiene/fire safety**
Kilburn House, Manchester Science Park, Lloyd St, M15 6SE
Tel +44 (0) 845 643 7225
www.shieldyourself.co.uk

Shiel Porter public relations
44 Hurst Rd, Horsham,
W. Sussex
Tel +44 (0) 845 643 7225
www.shielporter.com
Contacts: Ros Shiel or John Porter.

TLT Solicitors
1 Redcliff St, Bristol BS1 6TP
Tel +44 (0) 117 917 7777
www.traverssmith.co.uk

Venners Stocktakers
Essex House, Edinburgh Way,
Harlow CM20 2BN
Tel +44 (0) 1279 620820
www.venners.co.uk

Wellers Accountants
1 Vincent Square, London
SW1P 2PN
Tel +44 (0) 207 630 6665
www.wellersaccountants.co.uk

Index

A
Alcohol Wholesaler Registration Scheme 68
allergen advice 182–183
anti-discrimination policies 69–76
Ayling, Phil 94–96

B
bag-in-box cider 107
bag-in-box wine 154–155
bar equipment suppliers 217–218
Bar Sport 13
beer 84–105, 107–111
  bottles and cans 85, 99–101, 108, 109
  cask beers 87–93
  cellar skills 90–97
  craft beers 97–99, 108–109, 110–111
  guest ales and promotions 107, 110–111
  keg beers 85–86, 87, 97, 98
  legal measures 103, 111
  NLA beers 101–102, 104–105
  sales (UK) 2
  smooth beer 97
  specialist wholesalers 214–216
  tasting paddle 111
beer festivals 88, 95, 98, 110
Beer Orders 1990 vi, 1, 10
beer paddles 111
Beerhouse, Market Harborough 66–67
betting, small-stakes 61–62
Big Six brewers vi, 9–10
bottled beers 85, 99–101, 108–109
breastfeeding in public places 70–71
brewery taps 15
'brewery-conditioned' 87
brewpubs 14
business plan 25, 201
business rates 19, 24–25
  exemption from 1, 25, 27
Butcher's Arms, Herne 17, 20

C
café bars 159–175
  afternoon teas 164–165
  breakfasts 161
  coffee 165–168
  counter service 163–164
  lunches 162–164
  morning coffee and brunch 162
  soft drinks 169, 173–175
  tea and chocolate 168–169
Campaign for Real Ale (CAMRA) vi, 86, 87, 92, 94–95, 98
canned beers 101
cask beers 87–93
  Cask Marque sampling and scoring 93
  firkins 88
  gravity dispense 88–89
  KeyKeg 90
  polypins 89–90
  prolonging the life of 91–92
'cask-conditioned' 87
catering suppliers 218
CCTV 78–79
cellar equipment suppliers 217–218
cellar skills 90–97
  ambient temperature 91
  cleaning routines 90–91, 92
  flushing pipes 92
  hygiene 90–91, 92
  prolonging the life of the beer 91–92
Champagne, opening 150
children 74–75, 76–77, 172
cider 105–107, 134
  bag-in-box 107
  bottled 107
  carbonated cider 107
  on draught 107
  duty-exempt makers 106
  legal measures 103
  specialist wholesalers 214–216
  traditional cider 106, 107
Clancy, Stuart 94–96
cocktail bars 1, 3, 56, 122–139
  accessories 127
  bar-back 138–139
  gross profit 124–126
  ice 128–129
  mixers 137
  mixologists 126, 132–133, 137–138
  mocktails 175
  outlay and overheads 123, 126–127
  range of spirits 127
  setting-up process 123
  start-up costs 123, 126–127
  table staff 136, 137
coffee 165–168
Conisbee, Laurence 134–135
council licensing officers 48–49, 50–51

Index

craft beers and brewers 3, 14–15, 96, 97–99, 108–109, 110–111
craft distillers 125, 134–135
criminal activity on the premises 53, 58, 78

D

Daniels, Greg 22
Dare Café / A Bar Below, Leeds 130–132
Designated Premises Supervisors 23, 45–46, 52
Dinwoodie, Richard 108–109
disability-friendly policies 49, 69, 72–76
Disclosure and Barring Service checks 42–43
dogs 74, 79–80
door supervisors and security 77–79
drug use and drug dealing 58, 77, 78, 79
drunk customers, selling alcohol to 48, 70, 77

E

e-cigarettes and vaping 64
Early Morning Alcohol Restriction Orders 39
1855 Wine Bar, Oxford 152–153
employees see staff
Employer's Liability Insurance 25–26
employment law 44, 72
entry, right to refuse 69–70
environmental health inspections 185–186
equality policies 69–72
equipment
  energy-efficient appliances 191
  leasing 190
  secondhand 190

F

Fair Maintainable Trade (FMT) 202
firkins 88
food 177–197
  allergen advice 182–183
  café-bars 161–165
  environmental health inspections 185–186
  health and safety 186–188
  hygiene 44, 80, 181, 184
  kitchen design and equipment 188–190
  micropubs 178
  in small spaces 194–197

takeaways 196
training 178–181
waste disposal 190, 192–193
wine bars 143, 145–146
without cooking 193, 195, 196
fortified wines 145, 147, 151
Fozard, Ian vi–xii
franchising 12–13, 15
free trade 15–17

G

gaming 60–62
gaming machines 61
general drinks wholesalers 210–214
gin 124
ginger beer 102, 169
glassware
  cocktail bars 139
  micropubs 103–104
  washing 103–104
  wine bars 150–151
gravity dispense 88–89
gross profit
  cocktail bars 124–126
  micropubs 27, 126
  wine bars 144–145
guest ales and promotions 107, 110–111

H

hand-pumps 88, 89, 94
health and safety 26
  allergen advice 182–183
  in the kitchen 186–188
  see also hygiene
Hill, Mike 108–109
Hillier, Martyn 17, 20, 94–95
Holland, Dave and Nicola 22–23
hot chocolate 168–169
hotel bars 20, 122, 124, 126
hygiene
  cask beer 90–91, 92
  cocktails 129
  food hygiene 44, 80, 181, 184
  ice 129
  legislation 181, 184
  staff practices 92, 97
  training courses 180–181, 184

I

ice 128–129
ID 47–48

221

Inntrepreneur lease (Grand Metropolitan) 8–9
insurance 25–26
  Employer's Liability Insurance 25–26
  National Insurance 25
  public liability insurance 25
intimidating or violent customers 53

J
Jones, Gareth and Rebecca 40–41
Jones, Ian 21–22
Just Beer, Newark 94–96

K
keg beers 85–86, 87, 97, 98
  see also craft beers
KeyKeg 90
Kipp's Alehouse, Folkestone 74–75
kitchen design and equipment 188–190

L
leasehold pubs 8–9
leases 200–206
  buying an existing lease 200–201
  examining the books 200
  full-repairing 201
  grievances and arbitration 205–206
  negotiating a new lease 201–202
  rent reviews 203–204
  valuation 202–203
legal matters 55–80
  access and equality 69–76
  door supervisors and security 77–79
  gaming 60–62
  minors 74–75, 76–77
  music and live entertainment 56–58
  noise and nuisance 58–60
  pet animals on the premises 79–80
  sanitary facilities 68–69
  smoking 64–65
  sport, televised 62–64
legal measures
  beer 103, 111
  cider 103
  wine 151
licences
  liquor licences 38–39, 42
  pavement licences 49
  personal licences 42–43
  premises licences 32, 42, 46–49, 52–53, 77

  24-hour licences 39
Licensing Act 2003 38–39, 42, 76
lifestyle motivation 4, 8, 20, 21, 160
liqueur coffees 167–168
liquor licences 38–39, 42
listed building consent 37, 38, 41
live entertainment 57–58, 66–67
Local Development Framework 33, 35
Loungers, Bristol 170–172

M
Mandatory Conditions 45
Martin, Tim 17, 19
Matthew Clark 112–119
Mayes, Steve 50–51
metal pins 89
meze bars 146
microbrewers and brewpubs 14
Micropub & Microbrewery Association 3, 15, 17, 20, 96
micropubs 17–21, 122, 160
  food 178
  multiple operations 21–23
  outgoings and overheads 24–26, 27
  pricing and profit 27–28
  start-up costs 18, 20, 24
  see also beer; cider; legal matters; licences; premises
minors 74–75, 76–77, 172
mixologists 126, 132–133, 137–138
Mold Alehouse 40–41
Mulhall, Chris 152–153
Murphy, Paul 94–96
music
  cocktail bars 123
  copyright and fees 57
  live entertainment 57–58, 66–67
  micropubs 56–60
  noise issues 52, 58, 59
  recorded and broadcast music 56–57

N
National Insurance 25
neighbours, issues with 33, 35–36, 39, 58–60
Neil, Duncan 94–96
Nettleton, Rich 50–51
NLA beers 101–102, 104–105
noise and nuisance 52, 58–60
  see also neighbours, issues with

O

Old Transporter, Henlow 18
overheads
   cocktail bars 123, 126–127
   micropubs 24–25, 27

P

pavement licences 49
pensions 207
perry 105, 135
personal licences 42–43
   Designated Premises Supervisors 45–46, 52
   Disclosure and Barring Service checks 42–43
   National Certificate for Personal Licence Holders 42
   number of (UK) 4
planning applications
   change of use 32–38
   rejections and appeals 37–38
   smoking shelters 64–65
police 39, 42, 45, 49, 52–53, 79
polypins 89–90
Pook, Andrew 74–75
premises
   change of use permission 33–38
   leases see leases
   listed building consent 37, 38, 41
   neighbours, issues with 33, 35–36, 39, 58–60
   shop conversions 17, 18, 19–20, 32, 33
   structural surveys 201
   see also planning applications
premises licence 32, 42, 46–49, 52–53, 77
   application for 46, 48
   cooperation with council licensing officers 48–49
   fees 46, 49
   four licensing objectives 46, 47, 48
   Mandatory Conditions 47–48
   number of (UK) 4
   renewal 49
   review of and revocation 49, 52–53, 59
pricing and profit 27–28
professional services 218–219
pubcos (pub companies) vi, 10–11, 16
public liability insurance 25
pubs
   brewpubs 14
   closures 1–2, 4
   franchising model 12–13, 15
   free trade 15–17
   leasehold pubs 8–9
   tied tenancies 8, 11–12, 43
   see also micropubs

R

race spile 91
The Rake, Southwark 108–109
real ale see cask beers
recycling 192
refusing service 69–70
Reilly, Alex 170–171, 172
rents 24, 27, 123
   Market Rent Only (MRO) option 205
   rent reviews 203–204
   see also leases
Riley, Bronwyn 194, 195
Rogers, Steph 22
Room with a Brew, Nottingham 50

S

sales (UK)
   beer 2
   soft drinks 169
   spirits 124–125
   wine 142–143
sanitary facilities 68–69
Section 53 review 52–53
Security Industry Authority training 78
Sedgwick, Tim 195
services and suppliers 210–219
sherries 145, 147, 151
shop conversions 17, 18, 19–20, 32
Small Businesses Act 2015 204–205
smoking 64–65
   sale of tobacco products 65
   smoking shelters 58, 64–65
smooth beer 97
social changes 2–3
soft drinks 101–102, 169, 173–175
   artisanal soft drinks 174–175
   basic carbonates 169
   cordials 173
   diet versions 173–174
   gross profit 169
   mocktails 175
   sales (UK) 169
sparkling wines, opening 150
'speakeasies' 122

spirits
  opened bottles, shelf-life of 125–126
  sales (UK) 124–125
  spirits-based bars see cocktail bars
  wholesalers 216–217
sport, televised 13, 62–64
sports betting 62
staff
  cocktail bars 126, 132–133, 136–138
  costs 25, 132–133
  documentation 26
  door supervisors and security 77–79
  Employer's Liability Insurance 25–26
  employment law 44, 72
  health and safety 186–188
  hygine practices 92, 97
  managing without 25
  micropubs 25–26
  pensions 207
  retention 136
  taxis home for late workers 209
  tips 132, 208–209
  training 136–138
start-up costs
  cocktail bars 123, 126–127
  micropubs 18, 20, 24, 126
Storr, Ali 131–132
street, customers drinking in the 49

T

tapas bars 1, 56, 145
tasting flights 111
tea 168
tied tenancies 8, 11–12, 43
tips, staff 132, 208–209
Topham, Steve and Jay 18
trade associations, membership of 44–45
Trade Effluent Disposal Licence 193
trade press 45
training 43–44
  courses 44
  food training 178–181
  hygiene 180–181, 184
  qualifications 42, 44
  Security Industry Authority training 78
  staff 136–138
  wine training 146, 148
transgender customers 71–72, 73
Treacle Tap, Macclesfield 194–195

24-hour licences 39

U

utilities 191
Utobeer 108–109

W

waste disposal 190, 192–193
water, availability of 47
WCs, urinals and washbasins 68–69
  disabled access 69, 73, 74
  transgender customers 71–72, 73
Wetherspoons 17, 19
The Wharf, Potterspury 134–135
wheat beers 104
wine
  bag-in-box wine 154–155
  branded wines 144
  on draught 155
  fortified wines 145, 147
  legal measures 151
  opened bottles, shelf-life of 154
  sales (UK) 142–143
  serving temperature 155
  wholesalers 216–217
  wine kegs 155–156
wine bars 1, 3, 142–156
  corked bottles 149
  display and storage 149
  food 143, 145–146
  glassware 150–151
  gross profit 144–145
  wine list 144, 149
  wine service 148–150
  wine training 146, 148
women customers 143, 173, 174